Items should be returned to the library from which they were borrowed by closing time on or before the date stamped above, unless a renewal has been granted

Swindon BOROUGH COUNCIL

SBC.LIB 02

D0353750

online
share investing

A UK GUIDE

alistair fitt

FTyourmoney.com

PEARSON EDUCATION LIMITED

Head Office:
Edinburgh Gate
Harlow CM20 2JE
Tel: +44 (0)1279 623623
Fax: +44 (0)1279 431059

London Office:
128 Long Acre
London WC2E 9AN
Tel: +44 (0)20 7447 2000
Fax: +44 (0)20 7240 5771
Website: www.financialminds.com

First published in Great Britain in 2001

© Pearson Education Limited 2001

The right of Alistair Fitt to be identified as author of this work has been asserted by him in accordance with the Copyright, Designs and Patents Act 1988.

ISBN 0 273 65370 9

British Library Cataloguing in Publication Data
A CIP catalogue record for this book can be obtained from the British Library

10 9 8 7 6 5 4 3 2 1

This publication is designed to provide accurate and authoritative information in regard to the subject matter covered. It is sold with the understanding that neither the authors nor the publisher is engaged in rendering legal, investing, or any other professional service. If legal advice or other expert assistance is required, the service of a competent professional person should be sought.

The publisher and contributors make no representation, express or implied, with regard to the accuracy of the information contained in this book and cannot accept any responsibility or liability for any errors or omissions that it may contain.

Typeset by HK Typesetting Ltd, High Wycombe
Printed and bound in Great Britain by Biddles Ltd, Guildford & King's Lynn
The Publishers' policy is to use paper manufactured from sustainable forests.

about the author

Alistair Fitt is a professional mathematician and an amateur investor. He was educated at Dr Challoner's Grammar School, Amersham, and Lincoln College, Oxford, and now works in the Faculty of Mathematical Studies at the University of Southampton. He has published over 50 serious research papers in serious scientific journals; but that's irrelevant as this book is not about his mathematics but about online share investing.

The author is not an expert with many years' experience in online share trading in British markets. (This is hardly surprising as online share trading is so new to the UK that *nobody* is an expert with many years' experience.) Nevertheless, he enjoyed steady success trading the old-fashioned way (via the bank and brokers) and has continued to enjoy a profitable online trading career. Above all, the author understands the mathematics behind the markets, how all those jolly hard sums are worked out, what all those numbers mean and how you might expect them to influence your online trading strategy.

The author made (lots of) mistakes when he started to trade online and also learned a lot about how online investing differs from old-fashioned investing. If this book had been available when he started, he'd have gladly bought it and saved himself the trouble and expense of learning pretty well everything himself.

contents

read this!

Most books start with a preface or an introduction, but nobody ever reads them. You should read this chapter, though; it's only short. First, why 'A UK Guide'? As you'll find out if you survey the literature, there are plenty of books on online trading with a specific US slant. Some of these are aimed at fairly conservative online traders who may only buy or sell a few times in a month, but far more are aimed at 'day traders' who sometimes deal 30–40 times a day. Unfortunately there are hardly any books that deal specifically with online trading in the UK. Of course, it's interesting to read about how the DOW and the NASDAQ move and it's fun to read speculation on Microsoft's prospects, but the fact remains that people living on this side of the pond trade shares on the *London* Stock Exchange. As we shall see, things are rather different over here and not all of the *modi operandi* and tactics that apply in the US are relevant here.

The aim of this book is therefore to educate, advise, annoy and cajole *British* readers who want to take part in the great online shares game. This is not a book for professional traders; they tend to operate in fairly tight niche areas and in any case would be unlikely to be interested in a book of this sort. After all, if they're doing it for a living then you might hope that they had got past the 'book learning' stage. As far as I'm concerned we're all amateurs, or what my American friends would call 'turkeys'. Well turkeys we may be, but every turkey has its Christmas Day, and with a bit of common sense and planning you too can have your moment of stock market glory.

How is the book arranged? Perhaps it's best to think of it as being divided into three parts.

Part 1   The mechanics and facts of Internet share dealing; why you should do it, why you'd be mad not to do it, what you need to do it, what you should do before you do it, how you should go about doing it, where to do it, how much to pay for it, what to expect, how to avoid making disastrous mistakes while you are doing it and what to look out for.

Part 2   Some opinions and advice on how to Internet share trade *well*. As you may have guessed, this is the tricky part.

Part 3   Helpful (but fairly random) bits of information and some notes on some far more risky trading games that you might consider playing if online share trading is not exciting enough for you.

The first and third parts are largely factual; you can disagree with them if you want to but they probably don't contain any major mistakes. Of course, the Internet changes faster than any of us can keep up with so any pretence of total accuracy must be understood to be a vain hope: all that we can claim is that all website details were correct when this book went to press.

The first part (chapters 1 and 2) is meant to be read like a book (i.e. from the start to the end), and serves as what us old-timers (today if you haven't made a million with a dot.com before you're 18 you're virtually over the hill) call a 'primer' in internet share dealing. It's *not* an Internet primer and it's *not* a this-is-how-shares-work primer. It is assumed that you know the basics of what shares are, own or have access to a computer and know what it is to be online.

The third part (chapters 9 and 10) is meant to be 'dipped into'; you'll almost certainly want to add to it yourself and you'll probably find a whole host of more useful websites. You may even want to e-mail me (**adfitt@yahoo.co.uk**) to tell me about good new sites that you've found, problems that you've had or URL's that have recently gone belly-up and died, or 'free' services that you've used which have started bombarding you with adverts.

The second part (chapters 3–8) is quite different from the other two. It tackles the much thornier problem of how to *actually show a profit* when you trade online. Since I assume we are all agreed that the general idea is to make money, this is the guts of the book. I think that you should read every word of this book, but what I don't want you to do is to necessarily agree with all (or maybe any) of it. What you should take away from this part is some idea of how you ought to plan your attack on the markets, what the major dangers and pitfalls are, how different sorts of shares require different strategies, what sorts of financial data you might look for when you are considering buying a share, and, most importantly, how you might go about developing a successful strategy of your own.

We've already said that this is not an Internet or a share primer, so what do you need to know to understand and make use of this book? Not much. Granted, I've assumed that you're not a complete computer virgin and you know that you have to plug it in and that pressing 'return' can never make the machine blow up. There's even a glossary of Internet terms at the end of the book just in case there are a few definitions and terms that you've not come across yet. I've also assumed that you know what a share is and have some interest in buying 'em low and selling 'em high. That's about all.

Finally, in case you still have any lingering doubts, let me make my position crystal clear. *The second part of the book contains my personal opinions. I take no financial, personal, legal or any other sort of responsibility for them. If you stake so much as a button based only on my opinions then you want carting away.*

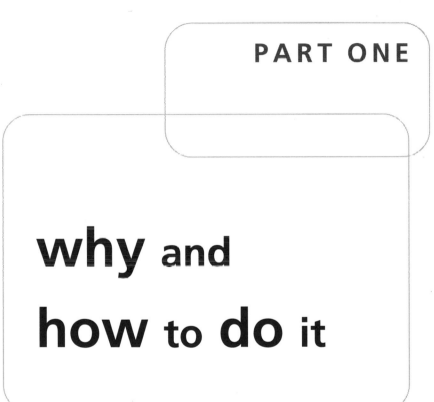

PART ONE

why and how to do it

why trade shares on the Internet?

Let me assure you that trading shares is much more fun than any form of gambling, and trading shares on the Internet is the most fun of all.

Why trade shares on the Internet? Come to that, why trade in shares at all? Let's start by answering both of these questions. Here are some very brief reasons for buying shares.

- Buying shares is fun.
- Buying shares is profitable.
- Buying shares is commonplace.
- You'll be old one day.
- The sooner you do it the more you'll make.

Now here are some very brief reasons for not just buying shares, but buying them on the Internet.

- All of the reasons itemised above.
- It's much cheaper than buying shares in a conventional manner.
- You have more control.
- The Internet is stuffed full of relevant information.
- Business and the Internet go hand in hand.

Those two lists were a bit breathless, so let's take some time now to analyse things in a bit more detail.

Why Buy and Sell Shares?

Buying shares is fun

Most people have a gambler's streak in them, and it used to be the case that if you wanted to give in to that delicious temptation then things were nice and simple. If you wanted to have a flutter, the national lottery, the football pools, the local casino or the horse (or dog) racing were the recognised major attractions for most 'ordinary' gamblers. Let me assure you right from the start that trading shares is much more fun than any of these, and trading shares on the Internet is the most fun of all. With shares, the 'horses' run all the time (or at least from 8.00 to 16.30 every working day) and just because one does badly for a bit it doesn't mean that you lose all of your bet. Shares also don't break their legs or get cancelled when there's a frost and it's also much clearer how to back the winners and steer clear of the losers.

So let's assume that we have to make an informed value judgement to decide the best way of gambling away a bit of spare money that has fallen luckily into our hands. If share trading is such a good way of betting, then how does it compare with all those other popular forms of gambling?

First, consider the national lottery. As far as fun goes the lottery must be near to the bottom of the list, especially as there's no skill whatsoever involved. It's just a pure guess and you *cannot* increase your chances of winning by 'skilful play'. For sure, there are many who swear by nonsensical systems such as knowing which balls are 'hot'. (So just as it's about to come out of the machine ball 13 pushes ball 47 out of the way, saying 'no, no you came out last week – it's my turn now'? Right.)

Believe me, you just *can't* change the odds.† We declare in conclusion that the national lottery is a game of pure chance (and, as we'll see, the rewards are poor).

So what of the fun of football pools? There might be some skill involved if you had to predict the winners of matches, but *draws*? Do me a favour! Be honest, how many people who play the pools really take time selecting their draws every week? However you look at it, the football pools are nearly as random as the lottery. As fun things go, doing the pools is a non-starter. Any pastime where the major thrills are marking crosses on bits of paper and watching the football results on a Saturday afternoon is unlikely to captivate the nation. As far as rewards are concerned, your average winnings are *even smaller* than in the national lottery!

Casino gambling is not bad as far as fun is concerned. You generally get fed and watered for free, and the gaming scene attracts 'a better class of person'. Time slips effortlessly away in the clockless world that is the modern casino and by betting randomly at roulette your fun lasts for quite a long time before you are finally and inevitably cleaned out. The trouble is, no skill at all is involved and you *might as well* bet randomly. For roulette, there can be no 'winning system' (unless the wheel is dishonest, which is very unlikely) and however you bet you're at the mercy of the house edge. Suddenly, casino betting does not seem so thrilling.

Horse racing is also quite fun, as there are certainly pointers to form. You can look at the beasts in the paddock, read about them in the programme and nose around the on-course bookies to see how much other people are wagering on them and where the best value is. It's also a colourful spectacle, and you can drink and eat while you are doing it. But how many people can tell the chances of a horse being a winner by examining its fetlocks (or whatever they do)? And how do you predict how they'll run on the big day? Not only is it still pretty much of a

---

† You *can* change your expected winnings, however, which is another thing entirely. Your chances of winning are so small in the first place though that this hardly matters.

guess, but it's a guess weighted hugely in favour of the bookmakers (though as you can see from Table 1.1 it's a far superior way of gambling than the national lottery or the pools).

With shares, things are very different. Things are hardly random at all and there are all sorts of general rules that are absolutely obvious. To take three examples at random:

- companies that make widgets cheaply and sell them for lots tend to do well;
- companies that borrow more money than they can afford to tend to do badly;
- companies that embark on aggressive expansion schemes often do either very well or very badly.

Of course there are many more of these general rules and many times when they might *not* hold. We'll be revisiting this in much more detail in the second part of this book. For now, the bottom line is that how shares perform is much more controllable. For the most part, if you back a winner it's purely down to your skill and judgement. For me, that makes it much more fun than any other form of gambling.

We seem to have concluded that most traditional forms of gambling are basically boring. That's not true at all with share dealing, however. When you buy and sell stocks, there's a real element of satisfaction in using a good dose of research, skill and judgement and, (let's be honest) probably a small dollop of luck to make a profit. With shares you really *can* use quasi-scientific methods to predict how things will turn out and you are at the mercy of far fewer unknown and unpredictable forces.

Does share trading have anything else to offer? Well of course there's the general profitability of the whole business (which we'll come to in a minute). Quite apart from this, however, one of the most fun things about successful share

103p	(Casino Blackjack: perfect play)
98p	(Roulette: Europe)
95p	(Roulette: America)
89p	(Horse racing: on-course)
88p	(Slot machines)
81p	(Horse racing: betting shop)
80p	(Bingo)
65p	(Spot the ball)
50p	(National lottery)
27p	(Football pools)

TABLE 1.1. *Average return for a £1.00 stake for popular forms of gambling*

trading is the sheer thrill of making money. However vulgar you might think this is, I challenge you to *not* get a terrific kick out of the simple boon of ending up with more money than you started out with.

Buying shares is profitable

To be more exact, it's profitable if you do it well. But exactly how lucky do you have to be to make a profit? To get some idea of what a basically jolly good deal share ownership is, let's first compare the average returns with some common forms of gambling. For every pound invested in the following forms of gambling, you get back (at least roughly; there are small variations) the returns given in Table 1.1.

I've ordered Table 1.1 so that you can appreciate at a glance which are the best and worst value-for-money ways of betting: as you can see, roulette is a pretty fair bet (though the house has a bullet-proof edge and you'll inevitably lose in the end) and the national lottery and the football pools are spectacularly awful ways of squandering your hard-earned cash. Why does anybody ever play the national lottery? 'But you could win a million pounds!' I hear you say. True, but what if you could still have the chance to win a million pounds and if you didn't *you got your pound back*? (In case you haven't twigged yet, it's called a premium bond. And you still play the lottery? Tut tut.)

Another striking feature about the average winnings given in Table 1.1 is that with one notable exception, none of the sums is greater than one pound; in other words, all of these kinds of gambling will eventually ruin you if you do them for long enough. The sole exception, casino blackjack, *really can* be played professionally for gain. Sadly, as many have found out, the problems in doing this include (i) you have to be able to count six packs of cards and (ii) if the casino suspects that you're actually managing to pull off this difficult feat, they're allowed to (and probably will) throw you out.

Now let's do the same sort of sum for shares. Figure 1.1 shows graphs of the US Dow Jones index and the FTSE 'all-share' index for the twentieth century. Index definitions come and go during the years and so some compromises have inevitably had to be made in Figure 1.1. The 'all-share' index is actually a combination of the now-defunct London & Cambridge Economic Services Index, the Actuaries General Index and the real FTSE All-Share Index, but this matters not one jot: any exercise of this sort will unerringly lead to similar results.

The upward curves in Figure 1.1 are obvious (and almost identical), and the bare facts are striking.

If you bet *at random* on shares, then each pound that you invest will make you an average of about 12 per cent per year.

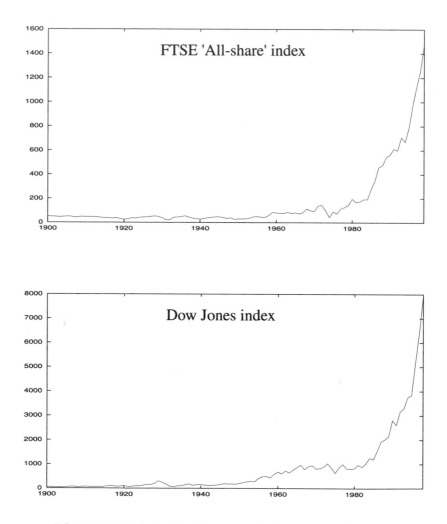

FIG. 1.1. FTSE 'all-share' and Dow Jones indices, twentieth century

Compare this with Table 1.1 and you'll see straight away why (from a profit-and-loss point of view) buying shares is so vastly superior to all other forms of gambling. It's also massively better than buying things like gilts (Government bonds) which have returned an average of about 6 per cent in the UK during the twentieth century, property (about 7–9 per cent, depending on who you believe) and bank deposit accounts and building societies (about 5–6 per cent).

Faced with this overwhelming evidence, we have no alternative but to conclude that only a complete lunatic would ever consider any other form of gambling if making money was the idea.

Of course, I'm not saying that you can't lose. The Embankment is littered with unfortunates who blew the lot on the exchanges. As we hear *ad nauseum*, the value of shares can go up as well as down. Just because the average rate of return from buying shares since the year dot has been 12 per cent doesn't mean that the FTSE-100 will rise by 12 per cent next year (or any other year, come to that). What I *am* saying is that if you want to gamble, at least make sure that you play the sort of game that mathematicians call a 'positive expectation' game where you can win in the long run.

Since we briefly mentioned premium bonds before, it's worth making one final random point in this section. The average return on premium bonds is between 104p and 105p and will shortly increase slightly. If you *must* wake up feeling that you might win a million this week, then buy premium bonds and *don't do the lottery*. In today's low-interest rate world, premium bonds are a good buy: it's no accident that many well-heeled and successful investors own some and it's also no surprise that one is only allowed to hold a certain maximum amount of them (currently £20,000).

Buying shares is commonplace

People have been trading shares for hundreds (possibly thousands) of years in one form or another, but just 20 years ago it would have been inconceivable that by the turn of the millennium nearly a fifth of all UK inhabitants would be shareholders.

Even as recently as the 1970s, owning shares (much less actively trading in them) was comparatively rare. Then, in about 1979, something happened: Mrs Thatcher. All of a sudden, capitalism was in and Governmental ownership was out. Electricity, gas, water, telephone and a whole host of other services were sold to the masses in an orgy of de-nationalisation, and suddenly any member of the public could be a share owner. This is neither the time nor the place to discuss the rights and wrongs of this (though some of us thought that we owned a bit of the country's water anyway, without having to pay for it . . .) but one thing is for sure: it had a profound effect on the share-owning psyche of the nation.

By the late 1980s, share dealing was no longer the province of yuppies, politicians and old gentlemen. Not only did ordinary people own shares, but they soon caught on the fact that there was an element of skill involved in knowing when to sell them, and that once you sold them, you could buy some more and hope to make money with those, too. The pace continued to hot up. The 1980s and 1990s stoked the ovens further as, one by one, building societies and co-operatives demutualised. Year after year, more and more of the population enjoyed the uniquely delicious charms of free money.

The fires of share ownership were burning brightly enough by the end of the millennium, but a positive inferno erupted when a flood of (often utterly preposterous) new issues in so-called 'dot.com' companies saw even fairly sensible people risking the family jewels on start-up companies whose only connection with the Internet was that the chief executive's auntie had once used a computer in a betting shop. Of course, some got rich quick. Many others lost the lot.

However you look at it, share owning and trading will never again be the province of the privileged few. Over 10 million inhabitants of a country with a population of about 55 million now own shares. Private investors carried out over 6.3 million share trades last year and more people traded shares actively than went to professional football matches. Ordinary people talk about share prices and dividend yields and nowadays, dentists not only ask you where you're going for your holidays, but also want to know your opinion on the recent volatility of the telecommunications sector. As we potter our way into the new millennium, share trading has become a national hobby, and you might as well be a part of it.

You'll be old one day

At least, that's the career plan. Death has its operational advantages but, like buying shares in companies who borrow more than they can afford to pay back, the downside generally exceeds the upside. Assuming that the grim reaper can be temporarily persuaded to look elsewhere for custom, how are you going to pay for your retirement? The chances are that in the next few years the state pension will be done away with, and if you want your autumn years to consist of a never-ending sequence of warm golden sunsets rather than a succession of bone-chilling frosts then you'd better try to arrange for some collateral to support you when you can no longer work.

Ponder this as well: in addition to the fact that inflation is likely to burn a pretty ugly hole in any savings that you have now, medical progress makes it likely that your retirement will be much longer than used to be the case. A long retirement is great, but if you have to spend most of your waking hours worrying about where the next water biscuit is coming from then the gloss is likely to wear off rather rapidly. You need to do something to cater for your old age and trading shares (provided that you go about it the right way) is one of the best things that you can do.

Remember too that when Mama told you all those years ago that a love of money was the root of all evil, most people had long-term jobs and carefully structured pensions. As noted already, they also didn't generally live for very long after they retired. In short, you had a job for life, got your gold watch, then you died. The average length of a 'permanent' job now seems to be about two years. So having some money to rely on while you're doing what actors call 'resting' is more important than it's ever been.

The sooner you do it the more you'll make

Do you understand what compounding things do? They compound. As they compound they grow bigger. Much bigger. Bigger at an amazing rate, in fact. That's why the earlier you start trading shares (at least, if you do it profitably) the more money you'll make in the end and that's why you should *start now*.

It's hard to exaggerate the difference that a bit of extra time makes to compound interest calculations. The whole point is that even though you may start with a relatively small amount and not be making very much on it at first, if you can sustain this performance and keep 're-investing the profits' then in a surprisingly short time, things will start to grow at an amazing rate. To illustrate this, let's see the effect of investing £1000 and compounding it with or without monthly payments. For simplicity we'll assume that the money is compounded monthly and grows at a constant rate year by year; the calculations could therefore apply to a building society account or a share.

Growth Rate	1 year	2 years	5 years	10 years	20 years	30 years
8%	£1083	£1173	£1490	£2220	£4,927	£10,936
10%	£1105	£1220	£1645	£2707	£7,328	£19,837
12%	£1127	£1270	£1817	£3300	£10,893	£36,950
14%	£1149	£1321	£2006	£4022	£16,180	£65,085
16%	£1172	£1374	£2214	£4901	£24,019	£116,717

TABLE 1.2. *Growth of £1000 with time for various interest rates*

Growth Rate	1 year	2 years	5 years	10 years	20 years	30 years
8%	£1706	£2470	£5164	£11,367	£34,378	£85,454
10%	£1733	£2543	£5517	£12,949	£45,297	£132,862
12%	£1761	£2618	£5900	£14,802	£60,355	£210,698
14%	£1789	£2697	£6315	£16,976	£81,239	£339,733
16%	£1818	£2778	£6766	£19,529	£110,341	£555,405

TABLE 1.3. *Growth of £1000 with added payment of £50 per month for various interest rates*

Table 1.2 shows you how much your money would be worth over various time periods for various growth rates that are around the 12 per cent that we discussed above for 'random' share purchases. Table 1.3 is calculated for the same interest rates as Table 1.2 and the same initial amount of £1000, but assumes that you also add £50 per month to your account.

There's no point discussing Tables 1.2 and 1.3 much as their consequences are so obvious:

- start now
- a small change in growth rate makes a huge difference in the final figure
- adding a bit on a regular basis makes an unfeasibly large difference to the final result.

Note also that the *total amount invested* over the 30 years of Table 1.3 is a mere £19,000.

Why Buy and Sell Shares on the Internet?

All of the reasons above

Absolutely. Need I say more? All of the reasons why you should buy shares anyway still apply to the far superior sport of buying shares online.

It's cheaper and easier

Now we come to the nub of the argument. Why should you change the habits of a lifetime and start to trade shares online rather than through a conventional broker or a bank? The answer is simple. If you look at the typical charges that brokers and banks make and compare them to their e-trade equivalents, then you'll see that there's just no contest. Here's a random example. Pressac is a small firm that makes electronic components for the automotive and aerospace industry. I have bought Pressac shares a number of times both online and through my bank. The breakdown of charges for two (real) purchases that I recently made was as follows.

- Online (E*trade): bought 1800 Pressac at 230p. Commission: £24.95, PTM Levy: £0.00, Stamp Duty: £20.70. Total charges £45.65, total amount spent £4185.65 of which 1.09 per cent was charges.
- At the bank: bought 1337 Pressac at 220p. Commission: £44.12, PTM Levy: £0.00, Stamp Duty: £14.71. Total charges £58.83, total amount spent £3000.23 of which 1.96 per cent was charges.

So in spite of paying the same rate of stamp duty (0.5 per cent) the online charges were nearly halved.

The difference is important when you sell, too. The total charges for selling the Pressac (for 255p – a nice profit) that I bought online were £24.95 out of a total sell price of £4565.05, and that works out at just over 0.5 per cent; to sell with the bank would have cost me £52.23 which is well over 1 per cent.

Now you might not think that a few per cent here and there could make much difference in the grand scheme of things. Alternatively you may have *really understood* Tables 1.2 and 1.3, in which case you'll know the long-term effect of seemingly trivial charges eating away at your compounded growth. Anybody who's been trading shares for even a few years will confirm that one of the biggest problems with the whole business is that *you get killed by the dealing charges*. Online trading allows you to minimise the charges and therefore maximise your profits.

Is it easier to trade using the Internet? Well to buy my Pressac shares through the bank, I manufactured a bit of spare time, sneaked out of the office, walked to the bank, waited in a queue for a while while the pub landlord paid in the morning's takings, told the lady behind the glass screen that I wanted to buy some shares, showed her my cheque book to prove that I had an account there, waited until the right person was available, assured them that yes, I had bought shares there before and no, I didn't want to make an appointment with their financial adviser before I closed the deal, waited while they made a phone call to see what the current price of the shares was, watched as they filled in a form by hand, read the form, signed the form, waited while they made another phone call, waited while they made the note out, went back to work, waited three days for confirmation, and finally waited a week for the share certificate to arrive. That's all there was to it! (Of course, I could only do this between 9.30 and 15.30, thereby missing two and a half hours of trading on the London Stock Exchange.)

To buy my Pressac shares online I. . . clicked a mouse button.

Now my bank tries its best, but it's not really set up for share dealing. To be honest, it would do better by not even *trying* to offer to buy and sell shares on behalf of its customers. Of course, strolling down to the bank is not the only way to buy shares. I could have gone to a broker. The process would have been largely the same though, and I still wouldn't have been able to check up on how my investment was doing at 3.00am on a Sunday morning. The whole process (and the accompanying charges) would have been similar to buying at my bank.

Faced with such incriminating evidence, you have to seriously wonder why anyone would ever use a bank or a personal broker to buy or sell shares again.

You have more control

Another top-notch advantage of online share trading is the amount of control that you have. For one thing, you can log in to your account at any time (day or night) to see what your position is, how each of your shares is doing, how much interest you have earned and what charges and dividend income have entered your account. If you have any doubts about the way that things are being calculated, then nobody has to be around to assuage your fears as the online help is there whenever you need it.

There are even bigger advantages to being online when it comes to the actual business of trading, for you can buy and sell shares with a simple click of a mouse button. Because it's so instant and you can see a preview of the contract that you're about to enter into, you know *exactly* what you are buying or selling, what price you are buying and selling at, and precisely what the charges for the transaction will be. How long would the bank take to send you a contract note? Three days? A week? If you buy using a real time Internet broker, the contract note is instantly created and may be downloaded and printed before the dust has settled on the shares that you've just traded. There's no nonsense about 'waiting for the money to clear' (a coded phrase that banks use to mean 'investing *your* cash to earn *us* interest') and you can use any profits that you've made to immediately buy more shares.

Regarding the control that you have, one point that should be made clear is how the price that you actually buy and sell at relates to the price that you see when you check your portfolio using one of the standard services (like, for example **www.marketeye.co.uk**). For one thing, most free portfolio tracking services and free sites which display 'current' share prices actually display the price as it was either 15 or 20 minutes earlier. The reasons for this are shrouded in business history, but basically the stock exchange to some extent 'owns' the prices and if you want real time share prices you usually have to pay for it.

Notwithstanding this, when you actually buy or sell shares the price on the preview contract is the *current* price. This means that you're in complete control and have all the facts and figures at your fingertips. Of course, it won't be the 'mid-price' that others will see; if you're buying it'll be the top end of the spread, and if you're selling it'll be the bottom end. There's nothing that you can do about this; after all the poor darlings have to make a crust somehow. In theory, you could get real time share prices free by constantly previewing orders to buy or sell and then cancelling them; this would be a bit fiddly and time-consuming though and might really give your Internet trading service the hump!

From an overall control point of view, the whole process is so much better than going to the bank or to a broker. As I've already recounted, I used to use the bank for share dealing, and to be honest the amount of control that I had over the whole process was miniscule. The bank was forever selling me shares at prices that I wasn't sure of; worse, they often (in fact on average half of the time) screwed up the deal anyway and made some mistake. Using a broker was a little better, but how often during a busy working day do you have time to call round to see them? What happens if they're busy when you phone? What can you do if they go on holiday (as brokers quite often seem to do)?

Even if you've been lucky enough to find a good broker, what do you do if *you're* on holiday in Mexico City when a key movement takes place? How do you get a message through, time difference and all? Another great control factor of an online share trading account is that all you need is access to the Internet and you can deal from anywhere in the world. Actually, it's quite a buzz to buy shares in the middle of the night from Hong Kong!

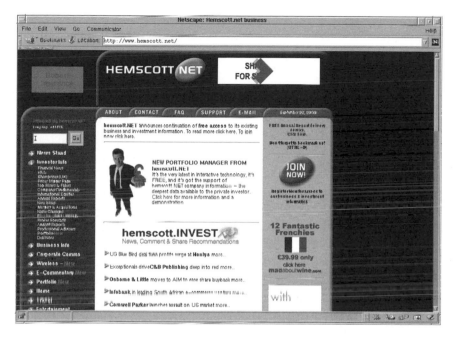

FIG. 1.2. The Hemscott web page – one of hundreds of sites packed with indispensable information

In summary then, the amount of control that you have if you trade via an online share buying account is unapproachable by normal means. For convenience, ease and general control, real time online share buying can't be bettered.

The Internet is full of information

One of the biggest advantages of online trading is that the very organ by which you do your dealing is also your single most valuable weapon for research. The final section of this book lists just some of the hundreds (thousands?) of websites that exist: each one is ready and waiting for you to plunder it for the facts and figures that will make your online portfolio a winner and your retirement to the Bahamas a racing certainty.

Even a quick look at the number of financial sites that offer business and trading information will convince you that probably your biggest problem will be too much, not too little information. Using all the data that you can pick up *in the right way* will be the subject of later chapters, but one thing is for sure; the Internet has led to a massive increase in the amount of information that's out there just waiting to be taken advantage of.

As far as amateur share traders are concerned, the emergence of the Internet is undoubtedly the biggest change that has ever happened. Just a few years ago, it was the devil's own job to get the information that one needed to guide one's personal share buying. Evolving a good strategy for buying and selling used to *have* to include things like 'trips down to the public library to look at financial data', 'phone calls to friends in the city to beg them to look things up' and 'reading things without buying them in W.H. Smith'. In essence, only a lucky few had access to the hard financial facts and figures that they really needed. Those clever fund managers were looked upon as gods, and when they smiled and told us that they'd had a bad year managing our portfolio, but there was nothing that could be done and anyway we wouldn't understand the complicated financial circumstances, we used to nod and congratulate ourselves for having employed someone so decent. No longer. The Internet has applied a huge and instant levelling machine to the playing field and we have virtually the same information as the professionals. And about time too.

Business and the Internet go hand in hand

The Internet is here to stay and even if you don't like it there's not much that you can do about it. At his acceptance speech after winning a second term of presidency, Bill Clinton remarked that only three or four years ago only nuclear physicists surfed the web, (wrong actually, but never mind) but now his cat 'Socks' had his own web page. More and more business is being done on the web and most companies have given in to the inevitable and accepted that without a large and well-thought out web presence they're dead ducks.

As well as allowing businesses to embrace the Internet to advertise and promote themselves, the web has already made major strides towards being a trading post itself. Take shopping. I'm told that some people actually *like* the experience of shopping. The crowds, the parking meters, the rain, the squalling kids, the rude shop assistants and the person next to you shouting into his or her mobile phone all seem to hold some perverse attraction. Well I don't like it. I hate the whole experience of shopping and I wish that I didn't have to do it. The Internet means that now I really don't. I can sit in the comfort of my living room and order food, clothes, computers, antiques and a hundred other things using only my computer. Of course, this appeals only to so many people and anybody that thinks that 'traditional' shops will die out completely is probably missing the point. But in more and more ways the Internet *is* business and its role in finance, commerce and almost everything else in our lives can only keep on increasing in importance.

This being the case, it would seem a trifle perverse to continue to do one's business by telephoning one's bank or broker or, perish the thought (as opposed to frying the brain), actually *walking* down to see somebody about buying some shares. You must have heard how fast the Internet is expanding. Will banks and brokers even bother to offer share buying services in a few years' time?

If you're still not convinced that online share trading is becoming popular and generally 'the thing to do' in the UK, then why not pick up the personal finance section of any good quality Sunday paper and give the adverts a quick read? Before the turn of the millennium the expensive quarter-page spreads that appear on every page used to be devoted almost exclusively to ISAs and managed funds. Today though you'll see iDealing boasting about how much cheaper their service is than the rest, DLJdirect promising a month's trading free of stamp duty for new customers, E*trade bragging about their recent commission-free trading day and most of the other online brokers making their pitches as well. Online trading is a rapidly expanding market and the advertisers know it.

Caution!

So now we all know why it's so much better to trade online than any other way, right? Well it would be being a little economical with the truth to imply that online trading only has an upside. There can be the odd problem associated with it too, and it's only fair to point out right now what these problems might be.

Some care is needed

Some of the (few) potential downsides of share trading on the Internet are to do with technical and operational things; some apply whether or not you're using the Internet. You've probably heard them all before, but I'll repeat them anyway.

- Don't trade with money that you can't afford to lose.
- Don't trade if you are in debt; clear the debt first.
- Don't borrow money to trade.

All of these are just business common sense, and have nothing to do with the process of actually buying shares. But I predict that if you *do* any of these *don'ts* then you'll regret it – big time.

If you trade with money that you can't afford to lose then of course you might be lucky. Consider though the consequences of being unlucky: not only will you feel awful about it (and probably your spouse and the kids will too), but you'll have a dreadful decision to take about whether you should carry on or cut your losses. Circumstances like this have led many a fine character to gory ruin.

Trading when you are in debt is nothing to do with holier-than-thou 'never a borrower or a lender be' morals – it's just a matter of simple arithmetic. Most debt these days attracts over 20 per cent APR and even if you are making say a fantastic 15 per cent on your trading (and therefore beating nearly all of the experts) you can bet that you'll be losing all of this and more in paying off your debt.

Exactly the same applies to the ultimate no-no of borrowing money to trade. In spite of the obvious rashness of doing this, more and more people are using credit cards, personal loans and even mortgages to borrow money to speculate on shares. In the US, this disease has reached epidemic proportions. At the last count, the total amount borrowed for share buying by private investors in the US had doubled in a year to a staggering £176 billion. If you find numbers like that hard to comprehend, then think of it as an average of £660 for each US citizen.

If you borrow to buy shares then the rate that you will almost certainly have to pay for the loan will be a good deal more than you can expect to make by trading, and so unless you are incredibly lucky, however well you do you will be losing money. Many investors (particularly in the US) got caught horribly on this nasty little barbed hook in the early part of 2000. With tech and dot.com stocks rising in a spectacular fashion, investors borrowed so that they could jump on the bandwagon. When the inevitable market correction came about in early spring, they faced a double whammy: not only had their strategy patently failed, but they had to sell what stock they held at horribly low prices just to finance the loan (rather than wait in hope of a recovery).

Security

Security is covered elsewhere in detail in this book (see page 59), and if you were pessimistic you could view it as one of the most serious potential problems with the whole business of online trading. Let's be sensible, though. It's undeniably true that you *might* be rooked but the reality is that the chances of this happening are extremely small. Don't let security worries stop you from online trading. Just take some simple precautions and follow the advice given in chapter 2 and you should avoid any major problems.

Your Internet connection

In the UK it still costs to surf (though there seems to be every sign that this may change soon). The basic position is normally that you can either have free phone calls but pay for your ISP (Internet Service Provider) or pay for the calls and use a free ISP. It therefore follows that if you anticipate doing a great deal of trading then you are likely to be making rather a large number of premium-rate calls. Of course, one way that you can keep your bill down is by doing your research at off-peak times and reserving peak rate times for trading only. Although the cost of your Internet connection is unlikely to be a major part of your online trading expenses, it's worth factoring it into any monetary calculations that you might want to make before you start e-trading.

Electronic meltdown

Just occasionally things go completely awry in the wonderful world of electronics and computer science. For example, 5 April 2000 was not only the last day of a UK tax year but also happened to arrive only a few hours after the DOW and the NASDAQ had suffered their most volatile ever trading days. For whatever reason, the electronic wheels came off the London Stock Exchange and the whole system broke down. Trading did not finally start until 15.30 and was extended to 18.30. The cabinet debated whether to extend the tax year by another day (though finally they decided not to). The market makers were left with nothing to do (though one presided over an interesting e-mail exchange about how he should best clear his blocked drain at home) and weren't happy about it. Conspiracy theories abounded. Had the breakdown been deliberately contrived to make sure that a tech stock sell off couldn't happen? Had aliens from space intervened? Chaos reigned.

This confusion was bad enough, but the electronic gremlins had worse tricks to play on private investors. If you had logged on to your favourite portfolio-tracking site early in the morning that day then you would probably have been greeted by some wild and totally inaccurate share prices. For example, investors in SEMA may have been somewhat shocked to find that their FTSE-100 stock had dropped by 56 per cent in the first minute of trading!

When this sort of thing happens, it's best not to believe anything that you see on your PC screen. Look around and comfort yourself with the fact that all the other prices have gone crazy too. Above all, don't be tempted to rush into panic buying or selling. Sit tight, wait for things to sort themselves out again and try again tomorrow. This is really your only sensible option. Be honest, you have neither the skill nor the experience to try to profit from circumstances such as these.

Partial cures for electronic meltdown

Although the e-meltdown described above doesn't happen often, it can be a major pain when it does. Other sorts of electronic glitches may spoil a perfect day as well, and while there's not much that you can really do if everything in the City falls down and the stock exchange's computers fail, there are some precautions that you can take.

First, don't rely on only one ISP. Set up accounts with a couple (or perhaps even three) so that if you try to get online with one service for that must-buy share and fail to get connected, you always have another ISP to turn to. A few months ago this would have sounded like a needless extravagance, but nowadays hard drives are so large and there are so many free ISPs that you might as well pick up an extra CD next time you see one and spend a few seconds installing it.

You could also consider opening more than one online trading account. If you need to buy and one of your e-brokers is down, then you can always use the other to carry out the purchase. The same unfortunately does not apply to selling shares, as the normal arrangement is that you can't sell stock that one broker holds on your behalf by using a different broker.

Oh, and by the way, don't forget to write down the telephone number(s) of your e-broker(s) so that if ever they're down for some reason you can still contact them.

The Final Analysis

What have we learned in this chapter?

- Share trading is more fun, more profitable, more worthwhile, more challenging and more stimulating than any other form of gambling. Soon it'll probably be more commonplace too. Even if you bet randomly, it's just about the most profitable form of investment that you can make and it's your best hope of providing for yourself in later days.

- In spite of all the advantages that traditional share trading provides, *online* share trading is even better, as it's cheaper, easier, more convenient, more easily controllable and more easily researched than ordinary share trading.

- What's the general public's verdict on online share trading? The figures speak for themselves. Even though online broking only really started less than two years ago more than 155,000 UK residents now trade shares online. There were 371,000 online share trades in the last quarter of 1999 but *close to a million* in the first three months of 2000. Since the Internet can only continue to grow astoundingly fast you'd be crazy not to embrace new technology and start to do your trading online.

WHY TRADE ONLINE?

- Shares have outperformed every other sort of investment year after year for almost the whole of the twentieth century.

- The number of active amateur UK share traders is growing fast: the number of *online* traders is growing explosively.

- Trading shares online is easier, cheaper, more reliable, more interesting, more fun and more controllable than trading with a bank or a traditional broker.

- Business *is* the Internet, and will be for the foreseeable future.

2

the mechanics of online trading

You are right to be concerned about security and some precautions that you can take are described here. Follow them carefully and you're much less likely to be taken for a ride.

The Basics

Now that you have decided that online trading is for you, how does it work? This chapter explains what you can expect and what you might want to look out for when you open an account and start to trade.

Let's begin at the beginning and start with the basics. Essentially all e-trading accounts work the same way and getting an e-broker is not difficult. Put simply, here's what you have to do.

- Get online.
- Download an application form from the site of the company that you've chosen to trade with. (If you prefer you can usually e-mail them and they will either e-mail or post you back an application form.)
- Fill in the application form and send it back. This will include sending them some money (usually a cheque) to open your account with.
- Wait until the company sends you your welcome pack and activates your password.
- Hooray! You're online and you can start trading. (You may want to transfer stock that you already hold to your e-trading account. You may also want to transfer money from your home bank account to your e-trade account or vice versa.)

All that was a bit fast, (though it really is that easy) so let's slow down a bit and expand on the steps itemised above.

Get online

This book assumes that you know the basics of 'the Internet'. To summarise though, you need a reasonable computer, a telephone line, a modem and an ISP (Internet Service Provider).

Although it's true that the faster your computer is, the faster the web pages that you access will load, computing power is not a key parameter as far as real time online share trading is concerned and a P200 or better (with say 32Mb of RAM) should be adequate.

The telephone line is a 20-minute home installation job (just add a spur extension to your original line) which even the most incompetent DIYer (i.e. me) can do. You may want to make sure that everybody in your household is happy with the arrangements, especially if your computer is upstairs (the commonest place to find one in the home). Houseproud landlords tend to take exception to holes in ceilings and walls; if all else fails then extension cables may be purchased for a few pounds forom your local store.

How about the modem? Most computers are now fitted with an internal modem. The modem allows your computer to understand the messages that are being transmitted to it down the telephone line and allows you to send your own messages; the best sort runs at 56KBPS and if by some remote chance your computer does not have one then they can be bought for about £50.

Have you noticed how the speed of everything else to do with computing grows at an astonishing rate, but the top modems have run at 56KBPS for a while now? There's a good mathematical reason for this, and it's called Shannon's theorem. Shannon's theorem gives an upper bound for the carrying capacity of a data link with a given bandwidth and signal-to-noise ratio. For a typical phone line the bandwidth is usually about 3KHz and the signal-to-noise ratio is around 30dB. Using these numbers, Shannon's theorem gives a maximum data transfer rate of about 30KBPS, so there just isn't any point having a faster modem. The only reason for mentioning this is that the corresponding figures for a satellite TV station give a data transfer rate about two thousand times faster than a standard telephone. Sometime soon, www will stop standing for 'world wide wait' and come to mean 'world wide whizzy'.

Of course, you need an ISP. This used to cost real money, but nowadays you can go into most supermarkets, record stores and many other shops and simply take away a free CD. When installed, this will give you a free Internet service (although you'll have to pay call charges).

Finally, while we are on the subject of getting connected, it's worth mentioning that the current sitting-in-front-of-the-computer style of online trading is one which may not last. WAP (Wireless Application Protocol) is here now, enabling anybody to access the Internet via a mobile handset. All sorts of figures are being bandied around, but most phone manufacturers seem agreed that by 2004 at least nine out of every ten mobile phones will have WAP capability. With WAP technology you will be able to trade from just about anywhere.

The application form

First, you should be clear that by downloading the form or requesting it to be posted to you, you are under no obligation to do anything whatsoever. After all, you might only be sniffing about to see which service provider suits you the best. Download more than one if you like and read them all carefully. Remember, you're the customer and they're the vendors who are competing for your business. Treat all small print with caution and make sure that you know *exactly* what you're filling in.

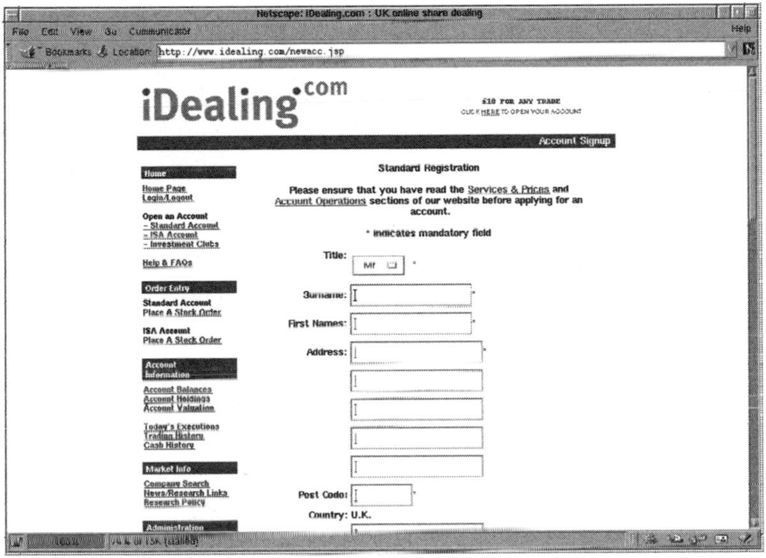

FIG. 2.1. The iDealing online application form

Completing the application form should take no more than 10 or 15 minutes. Of course, to open an account you'll have to provide your address and some of your financial details (like your bank account details and National Insurance number if you have one). This is so that a credit reference check can be carried out on you, but generally there should be no problems so long as your credit history is clear and you actually have the money in the bank that you say you have. It's also possible if you wish to set up joint and linked accounts; the application form should give you all the help that you need to do this.

Payment

The idea is that you send your e-trading service money, and they hold it an account for you and allow you to trade with it. The actual money is usually held by a bank in a special deposit account, and many service providers specify a minimum amount that must be deposited with them in order to start everything up. This minimum amount is often (though not always) £1000, so you may have to forget about the whole thing unless you have this sort of sum to start off with. This may sound a bit cruel, but in truth buying a few hundred pounds worth of any share is really hardly worth it once you've paid the commission, the stamp duty and the spread. There is good news too: most deposit accounts pay a decent rate of interest and your money will qualify for this.

You should realise that the moment when you actually send the money off is the moment when you've finally picked your e-trading service provider. Of course, you're not really committed to anything as you can wind up the account and send the money back to your home bank account whenever you feel like it.

Welcome to online trading!

After waiting a few days for the cheque that you've sent to clear, you're ready to go. If you find this short delay hard to cope with, comfort yourself with the knowledge that from now on as far as share dealing is concerned *you'll never have to fool around with cheques again*. When everything is set up, you should receive a welcome pack from your online brokers. Most send out a variety of documents and some include mouse mats, T-shirts, mugs and all sorts of paraphernalia. It goes without saying that you should spend an hour or so reading the documentation. Apart from anything else, if you rush to your computer straight away and embark on an orgy of buying and selling you might never get to know about all the neat and useful features that you can access on your online broker's site. Your welcome pack will also include details of an initial password (though not all e-brokers arrange things like this). Before you do anything, log in and change it!

Stock and money transfers

Of course, you may already own shares that you bought the old-fashioned way. You may even have old-fashioned certificates for these shares. Now that you have an online trading account, wouldn't it be a good idea to take advantage of it to centralise your shares and rationalise your assets? The transfer of shares to your online account can be carried out perfectly easily whether your existing stock is registered in your own name or held by another broker. It can take some time (maybe up to three weeks) to complete the transfer, so if this is your plan then you might as well set the process in motion as soon as possible. Alternatively you might like to wait a while before you make the transfer (just to make sure that everything's running smoothly – after all, you could always change your e-broker if there was a problem).

At some stage you'll probably also want to transfer money from your online account to your home bank account or vice versa. This is discussed in more detail below.

Actually Using Your Account

So your e-trading account has been activated and you're ready to go? Congratulations! Now it's time to get down to the nitty-gritty of actually using your online account. Go to the relevant web page (you've bookmarked it, of course) and log in to your trading service using your username and password. Now have a good look around. All sorts of information will be there ready and waiting for you to access it. What's more, much of it will be information that casual (i.e. unregistered) users of the site don't have access to.

The key subject of research will be dealt with later at length, so let's assume for the moment that all you want to do is to play around with the nuts and bolts of your personal account. Although you've already logged in once, you've only accessed the 'account holder limited' area of the site. To look at details of your account, you need to penetrate another level into the website and this usually means having to click a tab or button and then log in again. Don't think of this as a nuisance: it's for your own security. When you've logged in a second time you should be able to access all of your account details. Although each online broker's setup is slightly different, the options available at this stage is actually pretty standard. Essentially, the main alternatives that you'll be offered should read something like:

- **Trade;**
- **Orders;**
- **Trading History;**
- **Current Position;**

- **Account Activity;**
- **Cash Transfer;**
- **Stock Transfer.**

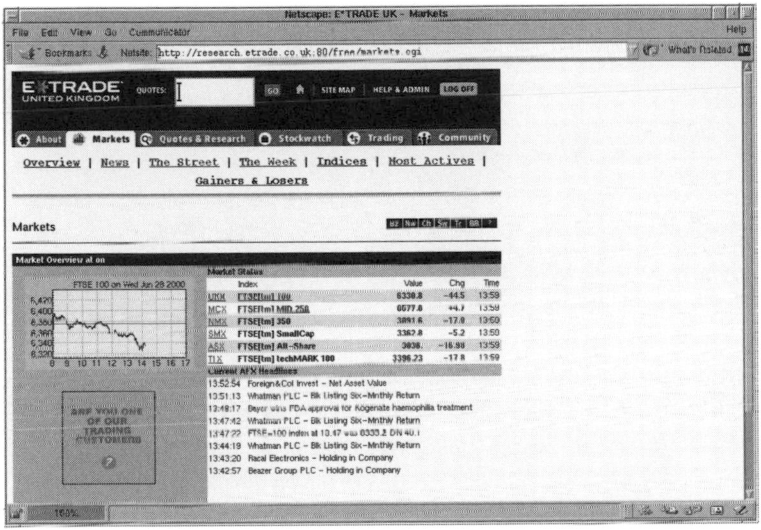

FIG. 2.2. The E*trade user account page after login (click on 'trading' to access your personal account)

You can do all of these things on a 24-hour a day, 365 days of the year basis, which is very useful if you're a busy person at normal times. Of course, shares can only actually be bought and sold on your behalf when the London Stock Exchange is open, which is currently from 08.00 to 16.30 (see also after-hours trading on page 59).

Now that we know what we can do with our account, let's examine each of these actions in more detail.

Trade

This is the key process whereby you trade your shares online. To actually buy or sell, you'll need to know:

- Whether you want to buy shares or sell shares (this may seem obvious but nevertheless you have to click a box to say which of the two you wish to do).

- How much money you want to spend and therefore, based on the current price, how many shares you want to buy. You should remember that when you buy that there will be stamp duty and some commission to pay, and that to purchase the shares you will probably have to pay a slightly higher price than the 'mid-price' that you have just looked up. Be careful therefore that you do not try to spend everything in your account because if you accidentally attempt to invest even one penny too much your share purchase will be refused.

- The EPIC code of the stock in question. The EPIC code is a three- or four-letter abbreviation for the stock (for example Abbey National is ANL, Pressac is PRSC, and so on). All the recognised e-brokers provide a quick way of looking this up on their trading page and finding the right code should be the work of a moment.

- Whether you want to 'fill or kill' or not. For reasons that are a bit hard to understand, not all e-brokers provide this service, but if yours does then it can prove very useful. If you click the 'fill-or-kill' button when you make out your buy order, you can specify a certain price which you want the shares to be bought at. If this price cannot be obtained for you, then the order is trashed and no trade takes place. The facility is at its most useful when you want to buy shares in a small company (for instance, an AIM outfit) and you can't be sure of the spread that you will be charged.

At this stage you're nearly ready to do the grisly deed. You should now be offered the facility to 'preview contract note' (or words to that effect). This is your last chance to make sure that you're actually buying or selling the shares that you intended, so it is important to check the note. Some EPIC codes are only one letter different from others and any mistakes that you make now could prove to be expensive. If you're happy, then the moment of truth has come and it's time to click the button to carry out the trade. Is it too obvious to point out that you should click the button *once* only? You may be surprised to learn that many online brokers include 'clicking the buy button' on their list of 'things most frequently fouled-up by the user'. So remember that with most online trading services *if you click the button twice you buy (or sell) twice.*

Assuming that your clicking is up to scratch, the trade should be executed. Some online trading services operate a 'panic zone' system when you click the 'buy' or 'sell' button. This gives you a certain amount of time (usually 10–20 seconds) in which you can retract your order if you wish. Other e-brokers deem you capable of knowing what you want to do in the first place, and just execute the trade without any fuss. One of three things should now happen.

- The trade may go through in the normal way. Your screen will tell you something like 'we have bought/sold on your behalf xxx shares in yyy'.

- The trade may fail because of some mistake that you've made. Typical examples of such mistakes are trying to spend more than you have in your account, entering the wrong EPIC code or failing on a 'fill-or-kill' order.

- The trade may fail because your e-brokers cannot buy the requested shares electronically (see page 51).

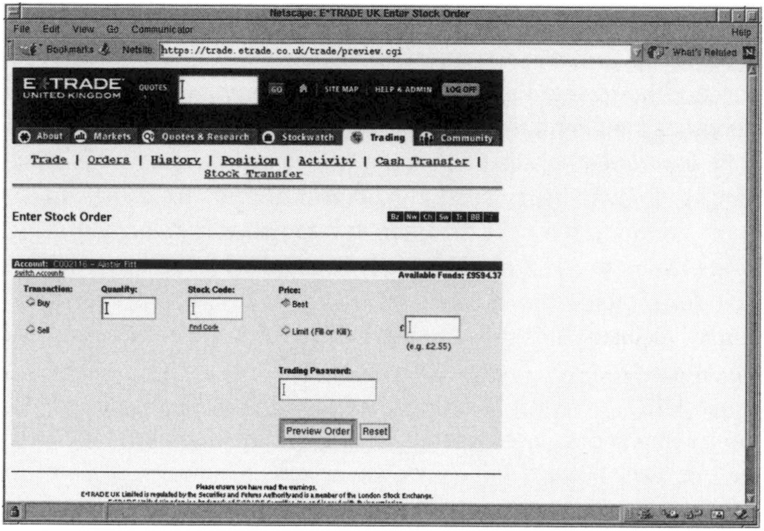

FIG. 2.3. The E*trade buying and selling page

Which of these outcomes is the most likely? You'll be pleased to know that the first of the above possibilities is what actually happens in the majority of cases.

Now that you've carried out your trade, is there anything else that you should do? Yes. We say it elsewhere and we'll say it again: when you buy or sell *print (or store) the contract note straight away*. Granted, you can probably get hold of contract notes from previous trades at any time you want, but it's really much safer to file it immediately.

Oh, and by the way: when you have finished buying or selling *remember to log out properly*.

While we're on the subject of actually buying and selling shares, you might want to know how the whole electronic shebang actually works. For instance, what happens to the share certificates and how exactly is the buying and selling done? Although the intimate details of how it all works doesn't exactly make a thrilling read, it's something that you probably ought to know. Essentially, the whole thing revolves around CREST, the electronic system for transferring UK shares from sellers to buyers and vice versa. CREST was introduced in 1996 to replace the slow, inaccurate and generally antiquated paper-based system that had been used on the London Stock Exchange for hundreds of years. The new paperless system is faster and safer than before, but still allows shareholders to retain legal ownership of their shares. The actual details of how CREST works are quite involved. As an online share trader, all you need to know is that CREST 'looks after' your share certificates for you and allows them to be removed whenever you sell shares.

As a company, CREST is doing very nicely, thank you, and clearly have plans for global (or at least European) domination. In April 2000 CREST sought to strengthen its position by cutting charges on the back of an 85 per cent profits increase in the year to December 1999. They even backdated the new lower rates to the beginning of the year. This reflected a massive increase in share volume; currently CREST deals with an average of about £200 billion a day.

Orders

No mystery here! Clicking this button should allow you to review all of the deferred open orders that you've made to date.

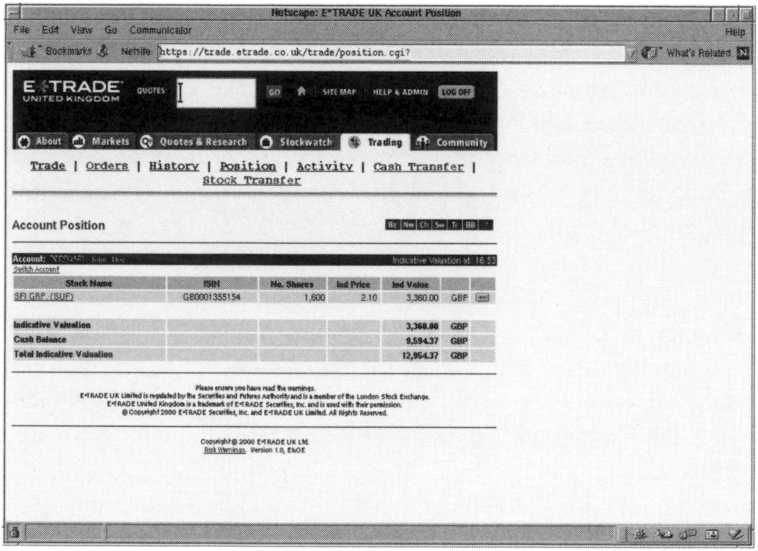

FIG. 2.4. The E*trade 'trading position' page – shows the number of shares held and their estimated value and the cash balance

Trading history

By using this facility you should be able to review all open and transacted orders separately. It should also give you access to the contract note associated with each deal. Dividend and interest payments are not normally shown.

Current position

This will be the feature of your online account that you will probably use the most often. It should allow you to access an up-to-the-minute account balance at all times which should include indicative values for your current holdings. Note though that the indicative values will usually be calculated using the mid price rather than the sell price.

Account activity

Your e-trading service ought to include some facility to give an instant statement of all the transactions that have taken place in your account over a given period. This can be particularly useful when you receive a form from the Inland Revenue. Your account activity statement should include full details of all cash and stock transfers, share trades, and all interest accrued, dividend payments and standing charges. If, like me, you're paranoid about keeping records, then you might well want to print this out every week.

Cash transfer

At any time you can either transfer more cash into your e-trading account from your bank account or channel some of your gains back to your own account. You'll probably want to do the former if either you run short (perish the thought) or if you decide that it's time to expand your portfolio. The latter is necessary if you want to actually *spend* your profits since the money in your online trading account is only available to buy shares.

Transfers from your bank to your online account are usually handled via a direct debit mandate which you supply when you open your e-trading account. There should be no penalty or charge for either of these transactions (although some banks may charge) and either should be completed in the normal three-working-day period.

Stock transfer

We've already dealt with stock transfers to some extent, and there's no doubt that once you're happy with the general service that your online broker provides it's a great deal easier to centralise your portfolio. If you have to transfer stock by sending off the share certificate, then it may take a few days for the whole process to be completed. You'll probably also be charged a small fee. Things tend to happen a little more quickly if your shares are already held in a CREST account.

We've just about finished dealing with the basics now. As you will probably have noticed, everything is very simple and logical and as long as you read carefully what's in front of you it should be almost impossible for you to go wrong. Other things can happen to your account and your trades though. The next section tries to anticipate some of the events that might leave you confused.

What Will My E-Trade Provider Do About ...?

Although there are minor differences between services, most online brokers will deal in pretty much the same manner with the following things that can happen.

Trades that can't be handled electronically

Sometimes you'll find that you decide to buy or sell a share but your e-broker will not handle the trade electronically. This can be very frustrating.

Before playing 'bash the-e-broker', it's only fair to point out that very occasionally, this refusal to trade electronically occurs simply because everything has gone belly up. If the computers that operate CREST crash or your e-broker's server has gone down then of course there's nothing that you can do except hope that the problems are sorted out as soon as possible. Mercifully, such major outages are rare, and it's really much more likely that your deal has been refused because of exactly *what* you've tried to buy.

The reasons why this can happen are rather complicated and may not occur on a repeatable basis. To cut a long story short, it's usually all to do with the number of market makers that deal in the share which you want to buy or sell. So what exactly is a 'market maker'? In essence, a market maker is simply a firm (which is often in reality a bank or a brokerage) that maintains prices (usually a bid and an ask price) on a given share. It is assumed that when a market maker declares themselves able to 'make a market' for any particular share, then they are willing and able to deal in this share at their publicly quoted prices.

The electronic link between your e-broker and the market maker is called a 'gateway', and it is through this gateway that clients' instructions to sell or buy shares are automatically executed and confirmed. Unfortunately, it is entirely up to the market makers to decide which shares they will support on the gateway, and they can remove shares as and when they like. Problems normally arise when the company whose shares you're trying to buy or sell is a relatively small one and perhaps only one or two market makers can be bothered to trade the stock. If your request cannot be matched electronically and no suitable market makers are available, then your online trade will fail.

When market makers advertise their prices, they sometimes also specify maximum deal sizes for some smaller shares. These maxima may be as low as a few thousand pounds. Trying to buy more than the maximum size permitted by the market maker is another reason why your electronic trade may fail.

Of course, normally you still want to do the deal. The few times that this has happened to me I've just followed the on-screen instructions and telephoned my e-broker. The trade has then gone through within a few minutes. If you do have to proceed in this way, then you should complain if you are charged more than usual: essentially the situation is a failing of your e-broker and they should charge you at the standard rate for the deal. Actually, most do.

Not being able to deal electronically when you want to tends to be a sporadic and rather rare problem. Although when it does happen it's mightily annoying, there are actually very few occasions when it can't be sorted out with the aid of a quick phone call. What's more, e-brokers are only too well aware that the curse of the failed e-trade is a major annoyance to their customers. As a result of this, most e-brokers are taking steps to ensure that their web of market makers covers as large an area as possible, and it may not be too long before all normal stock exchange and AIM trades go through completely electronically as a matter of course.

Dividends

When you own a share in a company, you actually own a piece of it. If the company does well and makes a profit, then it often (but not always) decides to reward its shareholders (who, after all, are effectively its financiers) by paying them a dividend. Typically, six months into the company's financial year there is an 'interim' dividend and at the end of the financial year a 'final' dividend is declared. Dividends are usually expressed in terms of the 'dividend yield' which represents the percentage return from the annual income on a share. Yields can vary greatly in size between companies: for example, in August 1999 Powergen was the highest dividend payer in the FTSE 100, paying a dividend yield of 6.16 per cent compared with an index average of 2.60 per cent. You can find the dates on which any particular company pays dividends on the 'key dates' section of their profile.

The real point is that if shares in a dividend-paying company are held in your e-trade account when a dividend is paid, the money should go straight into your e-coffers. You should be able to check on this by using the 'review position' (or its equivalent) button in your trading account. Most e-trade services also allow you to have dividends paid directly into another bank account if you wish, but really you might just as well let them pile up in your e-trade account. With most good e-brokers, cash dividends should be credited to your account as soon as they're paid. This means that all funds entering your account in this way are immediately available to use for trading.

Dividends are normally taxed at source (at the minimum rate) when they are issued. If you are a higher rate tax payer then of course you will have to pay extra tax on them. To help you (or your accountant) work everything out, your e-trade provider should send you a consolidated dividend tax certificate at the end of each financial year which contains the details of all dividends that have been paid.

Although dividends might not seem to amount to much, they can pile up surprisingly fast and are a handy reward for your loyalty to the company. It follows that you should make sure that your e-trading account is dealing with them properly.

Standing charges on my account

Some e-brokers charge you for having an account and some don't. Some also charge for things like processing share certificates for you or transferring money to and from your home bank account. There are websites around (for example **www.gomez.com**; see chapter 10) that comprehensively compare and contrast the relative prices of all of these services across different e-brokers, and you might like to look at some of these lists to decide who is giving the best value. Being a cynic by nature, I reckon that all e-brokers need about the same profit margin to keep going and make a decent profit. It's therefore normally the case that companies who charge you to have an account with them levy a bit less commission, and vice versa. Even if you spend time comparing all the charges it's pretty hard to see who is really the cheapest.

Whatever services pricing structure your e-broker has, they should at least keep you informed about what's going on. If there is a standing charge then it should be absolutely clear how much it is and when it's payable. You should be advised when the money has been deducted from your account, and all transactions should appear on your 'account activity'.

Interest on my account

It's a pleasant surprise to most people to find that many e-trading accounts actually pay a better rate of interest than they get on their own current accounts. It follows that if you have large amounts of cash sitting in your current account you might as well transfer it to an e-trading account (though this is not a problem that bothers me....). Interest is normally paid twice a year and the rates are often tiered depending on your cash balance. It's also possible to arrange for the interest to be paid directly into your home bank account, but as with dividends you might as well let the money be paid into your e-trade account so that you can trade with it.

Corporate actions

Here things may get a bit more complicated. Although dividends, standing charges and interest can be dealt with by your e-trade account in a pretty obvious manner, corporate actions may require some decisions on your part. Let's look at the most common sort of corporate actions.

Takeover or merger

A wide range of things can happen when a company in which you hold shares is the subject of a takeover or a merger. You may have to vote on the deal (with or without advice from the company) or you may effectively have no choice in the matter. You may be offered shares in the new company according to your current holding in the old company, or you may have to sell your current shares. Depending on the circumstances, a takeover or merger can be either good or bad news for the shareholders of the companies that are affected. Whatever happens, your e-broker should advise you by e-mail (and possibly by post as well) within a day or two of the corporate action being announced on the London Stock Exchange. If there is a decision to be made, then you should expect to be told exactly what the timescale is and how you should respond (sometimes an e-mail will do, sometimes a letter is necessary). If this sort of corporate action occurs and you happen to be unavailable for some reason, then your e-broker will usually implement default measures on your behalf.

Takeovers, mergers and the like can involve quite complicated decisions. The jargon involved sometimes tests even quite experienced amateur investors. A good e-broker should make strenuous efforts to help you out so that you know exactly what decision(s) you have to make and what you should take into account when you make them.

Rights issue

Rights issues require you to take action, so let's first understand what a rights issue is. When a company needs to raise some more cash (perhaps for a specific project or investment, or maybe to pay off some debt), one way of going about it is to print some more money. Doing this in a literal sense might annoy the Chancellor and New Scotland Yard, so instead, the company just prints some more shares in itself (rather than actual fivers and tenners) and sells them – simple! Now suppose that they've printed some shiny new shares: at what price should they sell them? You don't have to be Warren Buffett to work out that unless you give your prospective buyers a bit of a good deal, the response to the rights issue is likely to be poor. Since a poor takeup of a rights issue usually sends the share price heading in the direction of the basement, it's crucial that existing shareholders and institutional investors are enthusiastic. Traditionally, therefore, those who already hold shares in the company have a preferential right (hence the name 'rights issue') to buy a certain number of shares (for example a '1 for 3' rights issue allows shareholders to buy one new share for every three shares that they currently hold) at a reduced price (a purchase price of 10 or 15 per cent below the current share value is typical).

When a rights issue is up for grabs, your e-broker should give you all the relevant information and ask for your decision by letter or e-mail. You should get plenty of warning and know exactly when all the closing dates are. If you take up your rights, then the shares will be lodged in your online account and your balance will be adjusted accordingly.

Now that we can relax safe in the knowledge that our e-broker will sort us out as far as the technicalities of rights issues are concerned, we have a thornier question to ponder: should you take up your rights and shell out some more cash or refuse the offer? Whether or not to fork out can be a hard decision and may involve many factors. It's by no means true that a rights issue is always a good sign and buying more shares can amount to throwing good money after bad. One of the best ways to decide what to do is simply to ask the question:

'If I didn't already own any shares in this company but was offered them at this price, would I buy them?'

If you can see no sound reason to buy on this basis, then it's generally a good idea not to.

Scrip issue

Shareholders the world over love a scrip issue: the company gives them free shares! If, for example, you hold 100 shares in a company in your e-trade account and the company announces (say) a '1-for-1' scrip issue, then for each share you hold you get one free so that now you hold 200 shares. Unfortunately of course the market makers who buy and sell the shares on the exchanges are not at all impressed. The company can do what it likes with its shares, but they know that its basic value has not been altered by this cunning piece of book-keeping. All that happens, therefore, is that the share price halves to reflect the new number of shares in circulation. So your 200 shares are worth no more than your 100 were before.

Your e-trade account should have no trouble dealing with this: normally they should inform you what is going to happen but you need take no action (after all, who would refuse free shares?). One day you'll just log in and see that both the number of shares that you hold and the share price have changed.

Share consolidation

Sometimes a company has a 'share consolidation' which is really the opposite of a scrip issue. There's a general feeling in many market maker's psyches that firms whose shares are worth say 30p are not 'serious players' and describing a company as a 'penny share outfit' is still regarded by most as being tantamount to a bit of an insult. To make them more respectable, a company might therefore decide to consolidate, say, every five shares into a single new one. Just like a scrip issue, nothing has really changed: your e-trade provider should tell you what's about to happen and at the same time as the number of shares that you hold goes down by a factor of 5 the share price should just adjust by a multiple of 5 upwards to keep the value of your investment unchanged.

Finally, it's worth knowing that the *theoretical* share price adjustments that should take place as the result of a rights, scrip or consolidation may not always happen in quite the way that you expect. The very act of changing the share price may be intended to send specific signals out about the company, and this may cause the share price to change by unexpected amounts in either direction.

After-hours trading

It's worth finding out about after-hours trading as currently there seems to be no uniform procedure for dealing with attempts to trade when the exchanges are closed. As a result, not all e-brokers act the same way.

You know how it happens: when you wake up in the middle of the night, struck by a sudden flash of genius about why such and such a company just *must* go up tomorrow, the urge to log on and trade may be too much to resist. Unfortunately, when you click the 'buy' button at 3.20am it may not be possible to predict exactly what will ensue. Some e-brokers simply ignore orders placed out of hours and the trade will be nullified. Others will accept your order and process it as early as they can once the markets have opened. This can turn out to be costly, as the first (and last) few minutes of trading on the stock exchange each day can see wildly fluctuating prices and large spreads. Basically, you do not have control. The best way to get around this is simply not to do it Wait until the markets open and then do the deal. If you *must* try to trade after hours, use the 'fill-or-kill' facility on your account (if you have it).

Security

Are you suspicious at how easy it all is? Does the thought of dealing large quantities of your hard-earned cash with a few mouse clicks scare you? Are you just a little uneasy about sending a whopping great cheque to an address that you simply found on the Internet? If you answered 'yes' to any or all of these questions, then congratulations: you take security seriously, and that's a good thing.

You're right to be concerned about security and some precautions that you should take are listed below. Follow them carefully and you're much less likely to be taken for a ride.

Interrogate your chosen online broker

When you finally choose an online broker, call them up. Tell them that you're enthusiastic about their service, but worried about sending them money. After all, all that you know about them is that they allowed you to download some 'application form' from their website. If you feel uncomfortable about being so upfront with them, then you might like to say that a friend has told you that there are lots of crooked companies around doing this sort of thing, so how can you be sure that they're on the level? You might also ask them how many customers they have and how many times things have gone wrong for any of those customers.

The general idea is to make them sell their credentials to you over the telephone. If they're well organised and genuine, they should *expect* you to be asking these questions and have no problems giving you satisfactory answers. If they are hesitant, give you the impression that they don't approve of the implied slur against their good name, or generally don't go out of their way to help you, then fine, you've learned what you wanted to know and should try elsewhere.

Are calls recorded?

You should also find out whether calls to your e-broker are recorded as a matter of procedure. Some people hate the thought that any telephone calls that they make to the company will be recorded; personally, I find it reassuring to know that not only am I being monitored (which I have no objection to since I'm scrupulously honest, of course) but also that whoever is on the company end of the line is also being monitored. There has been more than one case recently when recorded telephone calls provided crucial evidence in the caller's favour that they'd been badly advised, so don't object to your calls being recorded; it's for your own safety.

Keep your password(s) secret!

Such an obvious piece of advice, but so important. A password is like a PIN number: the whole system is set up so that *nobody* should need to know it except you. If anybody ever 'officially' asks you for your password, refuse to give it to them and report it to your online broker, the police, the scouts and anybody else that you can think of. If you have a chance to use more than one password (many sites use a system with two or more) then do so and *make sure that they're all different*. Choose passwords that are eight characters or more in length and contain letters, numbers and other characters. Never use names or any words that might occur in a dictionary. And, above all, *never* reveal *any* of your passwords to *anybody*!

Insist on 128

Many things might influence your choice of online trading site, but whatever you do, you should insist on 128-bit encryption. This uses the 'public key' system based on large prime numbers and is currently the most rigorous commonly-used encryption standard. All sites that are serious about security should be offering it.

A 128-bit password encryption system is far superior to the traditional 40-bit standard (which in itself was actually not bad security-wise) and although it's obviously asking for disaster to predict anything in the world of computers, the current position is that there is no technology that is even anywhere near being able to decode 128-bit encrypted message by brute force. Actually, the story about 128-bit encryption has been a bit of a strange one. The software necessary to carry out encryption of this sort is export-limited from the US because of concerns about its misuse. Most of the best online share trading sites have now made arrangements to get around this however.

It's also worth asking your potential e-broker about firewalls, etc. A firewall is an electronic shield that prevents the site being 'hacked' from other links. Firewalls are very complicated and they might not be able to supply all the necessary details without handing you on to a professional. Normally, however, it's reassurance enough just to know that your broker has a firewall.

Insisting on the latest encryption systems and firewalls is all very well, but what about electronic signatures? Until recently, no matter how technologically advanced your e-broker was, they couldn't get around the need to ask for a *signed* application form. This has always meant continuing to use the postal service, and that it's impossible to open an online share trading account instantly. Any market researcher will tell you that generally folk are impatient. They want things to happen now rather than later, and the impossibility of opening an online account 'on a whim' has probably cost most e-brokers a lot of custom.

However, the long-awaited electronic communications bill was given Royal assent in mid-May 2000 and from July 2000 any documents 'signed over the Internet' will be legally recognized by the courts. The way is therefore finally open for seamless and paperless web transactions.

Of course, there may be teething troubles. It's not yet quite clear how easy it is to forge an electronic signature, and there have been no test cases in the courts. In summary, it sounds as though opening an e-trading account will soon become a lot easier and quicker, but for the moment you might be well advised to leave it to all those enthusiastic young cybergeeks to road-test the system, round the corners off and generally take all the risks.

Is your e-broker insured?

Now that you've decided to trade online, you're going to send some cash to an e-broker, they'll lodge it in an account, and if you do *very* badly then you'll lose it all. Well, fair enough. Shares can go down as well as up and we know the risks that we're taking. But what happens if *they* do very badly? The Internet is a great place for business, but just like other business environments, companies sometimes go bust. What happens then?

The answer is that you have a right to expect that whoever you choose to lodge your money with should have some sort of pretty bullet-proof insurance. The most common sort of protection is that provided by SIPC (Securities Investor Protection Corporation). This ensures (amongst other things) that customers' accounts are protected if your e-broker crashes and burns.

So whatever you do, don't be afraid to ask for details of their insurance. Without it, you could lose the lot no matter how well you trade.

Approve of transfer restrictions

Transfer restrictions mean that (for example) you can only use your e-trade account to transfer funds to and from a single designated 'home' bank account. This is for your own safety, and the system should therefore prevent you from moving money around between multiple bank accounts. You should also expect to be able to change your bank account details in only two ways: either by letter to your e-broker or by using the encryption-protected pages on their website. If you find that you are able to do this by telephone or e-mail it's a bad sign and you should change your online broker immediately.

Learn how to log off properly

As far as security is concerned, many users are their own worst enemies. One of the commonest ways of causing trouble for yourself is to take all the necessary precautions when logging in, but then to get distracted and surf to another site without realising that you've left yourself logged in (passwords and all) to the most secret corners of your trading account. That's bad enough, but if you then leave the room to make a coffee, well frankly you *deserve* to lose the lot.

Instead of risking leaving yourself as a sitting target, learn how to log off properly by reading the instructions that will come with your welcome pack (in fact read *everything* that comes with the welcome pack). Note also that the log out system should be set up so that when you press the log off button you should securely exit your account without closing the browser that you're using. That way it's not possible for anybody to access your account via the 'history' function. Other insecure ways of logging off include shutting down the computer, turning off the plug at the wall and frying your system by throwing a bucket of water at it.

Are there any other checks?

There should be other checks as well. The better quality online share trading companies operate their own automatic vetting programs that make sure that you don't try to buy more than you can physically afford, sell shares that you don't own, or try to trade in shares that have been suspended. Superior versions of these programs will also possess the capability to identify and automatically review 'abnormal' trading patterns and circumstances. Make sure that your e-broker is suitably equipped.

Assess the risks correctly

Yes, you should be concerned about security, but let's be clear: it's actually highly unlikely that you'll ever have any problems. Many people are unwilling to give their credit card number over the Internet even when the site is secure. Yet these same people happily proffer their credit card in a restaurant and think nothing of it when the waiter descends with it to the bowels of the kitchen and doesn't return for a quarter of an hour. How many cases of Internet fraud have you heard of? How many e-crime exposees have you read in your daily paper? Not many, I'll wager. Remember, millions of people now buy all sorts of products and services over the Internet, but there seems to have been an almost total lack of fraud. So be careful, but don't become overly concerned.

Check your browser!

Just one final thing on the subject of security: it would be a waste of time checking that your e-broker's site is stuffed full of all these hightech security arrangements if your own browser was full of leaks and loopholes. Different experts on Internet security will tell you different things if you ask them about browser security, but if you're using Internet Explorer 4, Netscape 4 or any higher versions of these browsers then you should be safe. If your browser came off the cover CD of a computer magazine and is not a standard one, then it's definitely worth paying a little more attention to your system security. Remember, pop-up windows should appear to tell you when you are about to enter a secure site (don't turn them off) and the letters 'http' in the URL (in the address bar) should change to 'https'. There should also be extra signs to indicate that a secure transaction is taking place (for example, the 'unbroken key' icon in Netscape or the 'locked padlock' logo in Internet Explorer).

Our American Cousins

Having dealt with most of the mechanics of online share trading, you might wonder why it's worth reading a book on the subject that's written especially for the UK. After all, aren't there already some books out there that deal with e-broking? The answer to this question is that there are, but most of them concentrate on the US market and the mechanics of online share trading are rather different over there.

There are superficial differences (like the fact that US share prices tend to be higher, typically $20 rather than a pound or two and the fact that the US markets are dominated much more by tech stocks than in the UK) but there are also some more major divergences as far as private investors are concerned.

One obvious difference is in the number of online trading accounts that exist. Several million such accounts have been opened in the US, many times more than over here. Overall though, the difference that bothers us most in the UK is that American online traders get a generally much better deal. First, they have no stamp duty to pay on share sales. Unlike us (who have to shell out 0.5 per cent every time we buy shares), American traders pay only the commission and the spread. Commission rates tend to be much lower too. Some US online brokers charge as little as $8 per trade, a rate that no European online broker is able even to get near to at the moment.

Many US investors also trade on margin, which is not generally allowed by UK e-brokers. Trading on margin allows one to buy shares to the value of much more than the money in one's account. Typically a margin trade will require you to have only 20 per cent of the total funds required for the deal in your account. If the deal starts to go wrong, then more funds will have to be deposited with the broker to keep the position open. The net effect of margin trading is simply to increase the gearing (or what the Americans call the 'leverage') of your trades. At the moment, the general opinion of e-brokers in the UK seems to be that 'there is no call for it' and as a result it's almost impossible to find UK online broker services that allow margin trading. This attitude surely cannot last though, and it probably won't be long before we're all margining away over here.

Another major difference between the US and the UK concerns the hours that you can trade. For example, although the NASDAQ and the NYSE nominally close at 16.00, live dealing is actually permitted (via a system of matched trades) until 18.30. Of course, all the usual liquidity problems can apply and are more likely to be a problem 'out of hours'. Currently there seems be a general opinion that eventually the NASDAQ will move towards 24-hour trading and if this happens, God help us all.

The bottom line is that 'rip-off Britain' seems to be at it again. Remember though, the more online accounts that are opened in the UK and elsewhere in Europe, the greater the competition will be. This will bring down commission rates and bring the consumer many other benefits. So complain, make a fuss, question everything and vote with your feet.

What About The Tax Situation?

While we're on the subject of the mechanics of online share trading, we might as well think about some of the more boring aspects of Internet dealing. The more successful you are the more you're going to have to think about how your burgeoning fortune will affect your tax situation. Most amateur (and professional, come to that) British share traders feel that they're pretty hard done by when it comes to taxation. My American and European friends are shocked by the heavy taxes that we pay on capital gains in the UK, but for the moment there's not much that you can do about it except at least to understand what you're liable for and how the system works.

The first observation that should be made is that tax is a private matter. For the definitive story you should always consult your financial adviser, accountant and/or the tax office. With this caveat understood, let's look briefly at the basics of the tax situation.

The first thing to understand is how income from shares is treated. You might think that since dividends are something that arise directly *from* shares, they are treated more or less the same way: unfortunately this is not the case. In essence, dividends are counted as income but any money that you make from buying and selling shares on the Internet (or anywhere else, for that matter) is liable for capital gains tax (CGT).

Whenever you are paid a dividend you also receive a 'tax credit'. This may either be sent to your address along with a dividend cheque or be credited directly to your e-trade account. At the end of each financial year, your e-trade provider should send you a consolidated tax statement which details your exact dividend position; then you'll be able to fill in that tax form and keep the Inland Revenue happy. Dividends are always taxed at source and the current rate is 10 per cent. Before you ever receive any money, you'll have paid this. For dividends, your tax situation will only become more complicated if you are a higher-rate tax payer. (The trigger income for higher-rate taxation was £28,000 in 1999–2000 and £28,400 in 2000–2001.) If this happy situation applies to you, then you'll be liable for extra tax on the proportion of the dividends that exceed your lower rate tax allowance.

All clear so far? Very well then, suppose we now consider the profit that you make from the sale of your shares. In 1999–2000 the CGT allowance was £7100, and this was raised to £7200 for the year 2000–2001. The CGT allowance is basically the amount of profit that you're allowed to make before you have to pay tax on your ill-gotten gains. So if you're set to make £10,000 profit next year, then well done! But you'll have to pay tax on nearly £3000 of it. Note that you may *hold* as many shares as you like: the proceeds from them only become liable to CGT *when you sell them* and (in tax-speak) 'realise your capital gain'. Of course, if you sell shares at a loss then you can set this against your gain and subtract your loss. It therefore follows that there are some occasions when it makes sense to get rid of a share that's been a complete dog just before the end of the tax year to avoid having to pay CGT. The catch is that CGT cannot generally be carried forward from year to year, so if, for instance, you make £14,000 this year and nothing next year you'll be clobbered much harder than if you'd made an even £7000 for two years running.

Although this is the basic position, things can get a lot more complicated. CGT must be paid on a range of other gains (for instance, the sale of a second home) and there are various 'reliefs' that may allow you to partially carry a gain forward to the next year. There is also the famed (more for its complexity than its generosity) 'taper relief' which was introduced partly to try to encourage people to hold shares for long periods of time. In the March 2000 budget, under the auspices of taper relief the Chancellor improved the tax situation for shares bought on AIM. From April 2000 taper relief on CGT (which could cut the tax due from 40 per cent to 10 per cent) will apply to AIM shares as long as they are held for at least four years. This used only to apply to employees who bought shares in their own AIM-quoted companies. If we were to discuss the ins and outs of taper relief and its long list of relatives here then this book would become unmanageably heavy, and you'd fall asleep (presuming you're still awake at this point). If the details of all this seem massively exciting to you though, why not pop along to your local tax office and pick up a (free) copy of 'Personal Taxpayer Series CGT1'. Then you can be further thrilled in the privacy of your own home.

What you've just had to wade through are the current facts, but how does this all relate to online trading? To tell the truth, it's really surprisingly difficult to find out. Anxious to know, I bit the bullet and made an appointment with a tax inspector. Although the finer points of the way in which CGT is applied to online trading still seem to be being developed, it appears that you realise your capital gain as soon as shares are sold and the money is credited (albeit electronically) to your account. Unfortunately this means that you can forget any grand schemes that you may have been cooking up of evading CGT by judiciously transferring just the right amount of cash to your standard bank account on the last day of the tax year. What may be required as 'proof' for the taxman seems much more uncertain. The problem is that it's pretty obvious that when you download your statements it would not be a difficult matter to illegally edit them to your advantage. There does not seem to have been a test case relating to matters like these so far and the Inland Revenue may not yet have caught up with all the issues that they will eventually have to face. I like to be completely straight with my tax affairs and not knowing exactly what's happening does not tend to make things any easier.

My interview with the tax inspector started to take a decidedly downward turn when I asked for clarification about what tax I was liable for if I bought shares on the UK stock market using a US e broker from a terminal in Hong Kong. If the money is held in a nominee account in Chicago, but I arrange for the dividends to be paid to my London account, whose tax laws do I have to obey, and when do I have to obey them? Surprisingly, the 'advice' that I received from the tax office was that they could give me no advice. Then I asked them about the legality of deferring my capital gains position until the next year by taking one long and one short position in an online future and using the one that did badly to realise a capital loss. At this point I was aware of (a no doubt more senior) 'somebody else' being present in the room, after which the interview was soon terminated (this really happened). My conclusion is therefore that the tax people really do not yet know the answers to these questions. Their official (and rather remarkable) position is that they will not answer 'hypothetical' questions and if I want to engage in such activities then I should fill all the details in on my tax form and they will examine it and tell me whether it's legal or not!

Each year 10 per cent of taxpayers are selected 'randomly' for especially detailed investigation. The cynic in me says that this might just be the year that I will be picked for this special honour. A complete coincidence, of course.

Summary

As I hope you are now convinced, opening an online trading account is both quick and easy. Keeping track of what's happening to the money in your online account is easy too and the business of buying and selling shares couldn't be simpler. The first part of this book is therefore at an end. Now that we know the nuts and bolts of why and how to e-trade, we must turn to the far less trivial question of how to do it well.

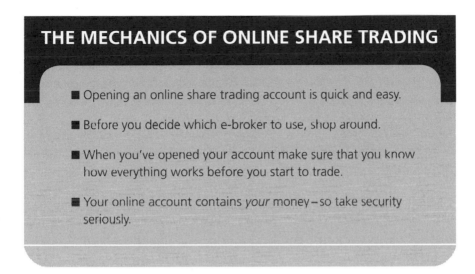

THE MECHANICS OF ONLINE SHARE TRADING

■ Opening an online share trading account is quick and easy.

■ Before you decide which e-broker to use, shop around.

■ When you've opened your account make sure that you know how everything works before you start to trade.

■ Your online account contains *your* money – so take security seriously.

PART TWO

how to do it well

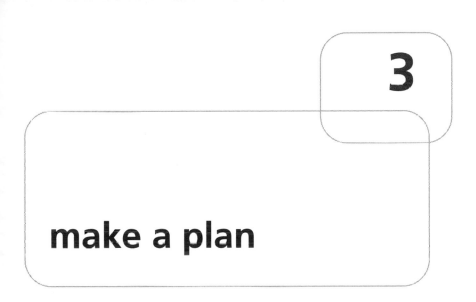

3

make a plan

A plan isn't a set of rules that you're never allowed to break. Neither is it a set of vague statements of intent that you almost never adhere to. The best plans are something in between.

Make a Plan. I'll say it again, in case you didn't hear the first time: *make a plan*. Even professional traders like Warren Buffett (one of the three richest men in the world) don't know what the markets are doing most of the time, so what hope have you got of succeeding if you don't at least *try* to give your Internet share trading some structure? If you decide to proceed on a 'seat of the pants' basis then of course you may be lucky. You may even be lucky for a while. In the long run though you'll probably end up losing money, and with the average gains that the stock exchange ought to offer, that's a crime.

The decision to make a plan *before* you make your first online trade is a key step in your e-trading career. The plan that you come up with might not be (in fact almost certainly won't be) 100 per cent correct, but merely by the act of thinking about it you will have established the basis of a *modus operandi* which will bring much gold to you in the long run.

There are many types of plan that you could make: some are the right sort, some are the wrong sort and some are just plain dumb. People make plans for all sorts of financial, fiscal and even gambling exploits but the normal problem is that they are unable to distinguish between a proper plan, a wish-list, a simple 'statement of intent' and an unstructured set of random rules. Half the battle is knowing what sort of thing it's reasonable to have in your plan. Ultimately you'll build your own plan, which will be informed and changed as your experience increases. In this chapter the idea is to give you some idea about where to start, what to consider, and the mistakes to avoid.

What A Plan Isn't

A plan isn't a set of rules that you're never allowed to break. On the other hand, a plan isn't a set of vague statements of intent that you almost never adhere to. The best plans are something in between. There *are* online traders (and day traders – we'll come them later) who operate according to completely rigid and fixed plans that work automatically and require no extra thought, and some of them claim to enjoy considerable success. The trouble is that none of these plans seems to work over a long period. Anyway, if you want it all to be automatic then you might as well programme a computer to do it (as happens for FTSE-100 tracker funds and the like) or hire a fund manager (who will almost certainly perform worse than the computer).

Another thing that a plan isn't is a wish list. The whole idea is that it should be practical enough to help you to make difficult decisions but flexible enough to allow you to change it and fine tune it from time to time. A plan that consists of vague statements like 'I plan to show a return of 40 per cent' isn't a plan, it's a (vain) hope.

A plan isn't something that you get from this, or any other book. You may get some ideas on how to make a skeleton for your plan from this book, but it should be something that develops over time and changes to suit your needs. Things that you read in other books and observe for yourself may eventually figure in your own personal plan, Above all though, your investing and your plan for doing it should say something about *you*. It would be unbearably pretentious to talk about 'expressing yourself' and 'artistic fulfilment', but in the end how you choose to conduct yourself in the stock market should be something that makes you feel good about yourself.

What A Plan Is

Once you have decided to make a plan (and a jolly good thing too), you have to decide what it's going to consist of. I find it easiest to divide my plan into three sections:

- general strategy;
- buying shares;
- selling shares.

General strategy deals with the sorts of things that you're going to base your tactics around. How much money are you going to tie up in e-trading? What sectors are you interested in? How often do you plan to trade? Does dividend yield bother you? How much risk are you prepared to take? The answers to all these questions and many more besides should be in the 'general strategy' section of your plan.

Buying shares is the part of the plan that helps you to actually decide to click the 'buy' button (just once, we hope...). What finally makes you do it? What price do you buy at? When do you buy?

Selling shares is the hardest part of the plan. If anybody breezily tells you 'shares are easy, you just buy low and sell them once they're high' then the chances are that they're talking out of the back of their head. You'll soon find out that knowing when to sell is the hardest skill of all: in the great shareowners' jungle, it's what in the end separates the tigers from the antelopes that they prey on.

Some Things That Might Be In Your Plan

I've dealt with the structure of your plan, but (like a politician explaining the budget) it's easy to waffle on in general terms about 'having a plan' and much harder to actually formulate one that has some chance of working. Many of the points introduced below will be discussed in more detail in later chapters, but here is an initial list (subdivided for convenience into 'general strategy', 'buying' and 'selling') of things that you may like to consider including.

General strategy

How much will I spend?

How much to spend is very much a matter for the individual, but for goodness' sake be sensible. It sounds so obvious to say that you should only ever invest money that you can afford to lose, but every day investors fall by the wayside because they get themselves in too deep.

A good example of the sort of situation that people can get themselves into happened a great deal during the 'millennium' winter of 1999/2000. The temporary madness that afflicted Internet shares was at its height and it seemed that you only had to open the newspaper to read how easy it was to become a millionaire and how many people had made fortunes buying stocks that rose by a factor of ten the next day. Some irresponsible newspapers started to press the case that 'it was too big a risk not to be in Internet stocks' and many lost far more than they could afford to by backing companies that had never made a profit in their history.

The ubiquitous warning that 'the value of shares can go down as well as up' is as relevant today as it ever was, and if you risk an amount of money that would materially affect your lifestyle if you lost it, then you're probably heading for trouble. It's safest to start off with a certain amount in your e-trade account and vow that if you lose the lot, then you'll stop there and then. Otherwise you may just be throwing good money after bad. As a general guide, I would be unhappy if my e-trade account contained more than a fifth of my total assets (not including the house). You'll probably have your own views on this. Just be sure that you think carefully about them before and not after you start trading.

What should I do before I start?

Given that you've already thought pretty hard about how much you're going to invest in your e-trading career, there are a couple of things that you should definitely do before you start trading for real.

First, you should get to know your way about your online broker's website. Like finding the tap on the rising main when you first move into a house, the time to learn where everything is and who you should contact in case of trouble is *not* when you're desperately trying to sell a flagging stock and something's wrong with the site.

Second, you should be enthusiastic about using the 'fantasy portfolio' facilities that most online traders provide. This allows you to have a dry run before actually risking any real cash. Even if you only play with this for a week or so, it will teach you a lot about how the system works. Do things like 'accidentally' buying too much of a stock: does it complain? What happens if you try to sell just after the markets close? What happens if you accidentally click the 'buy' button twice? (It bears repeating that with most online trading services, clicking twice buys twice.) How long does it take for everything to be settled? What happens if you try to buy an AIM or an OFEX share? Checking these things at the onset can save you lots of hassle later on. Of course, you need not limit your fooling around with fantasy portfolios to before you start trading for real. One very successful amateur online trader (and football lover) that I know runs a whole 'reserve team' of fantasy portfolios to test out what she calls 'up-and-coming players that may get their chance in the first team one day'. Her reserve team includes an experimental high-yield portfolio, a recovery portfolio and a 'nutters' portfolio of highly volatile companies. Experiment as much as you can: it's fun, educational and your mistakes will cost nothing except pride.

Is this a solo effort?

Let's get this sorted out straight away – who's in the game? Is it just me, or will my beloved better half also be involved? More importantly, will she cough up any cash out of her bulging 'emergency account' to put into the venture, and if she does, what say will she have in what and when I (sorry we) buy and sell? If a friend wants to give me 500 quid to invest for him and his wife, will he have access to the online trading account? Will she? What documentation will they require? What happens if I die?

The general rule here is that if you're contemplating anything *but* a solo venture, then you'd jolly well better get the details sorted out, agreed on and written down before you start. If this seems too obvious to mention, just think back to some of the fiascos that the national lottery has been responsible for when syndicates have won large sums. Friendships and families can be torn apart by disagreements. So get it right *before you start*.

Of course, you might be thinking of forming an online investors' club. If you are, then your commitment to club organisation should be structured and well thought out. As usual, the web can come to your rescue here. An organisation called ProShare acts as an umbrella organisation for investment clubs in the UK and will provide a manual to help you set up your club for about £25. Check them out on **www.proshare.org.uk** and while you're about it have a look at some of the many excellent sites that are devoted to share clubs.

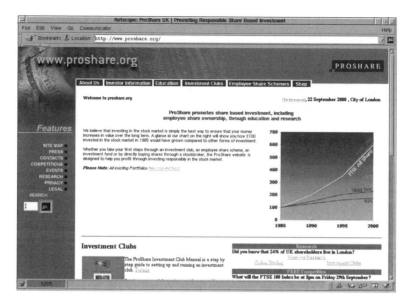

FIG. 3.1. The ProShare website

The 'Zulu principle'

The legendary Jim Slater (who in his day was a share picker of extraordinary vision) explains in his book *Beyond the Zulu Principle* the advantages of becoming an expert in a particular area by observing that, after his wife had read a four-page article in *Reader's Digest* on Zulus she knew more than him about Zulus. If she had then borrowed all the books in the public library on Zulus, he argues, then she would have become the leading expert on Zulus in Surrey. Mr Slater's view of academic research and its reliance on the material contained in public libraries may be somewhat questionable, but you can see what he meant. The idea is that instead of trying to keep track of hundreds of different companies that all make different products and trade in different ways, you should instead concentrate on one particular sort of share or sector and try to make yourself an expert in this narrow field.

There is certainly no doubt that if you follow all of the shares in one particular sector for a while, you tend to get a very valuable overall picture of what's going on, and you may like to consider 'Zuluing it' in this fashion. It's worth thinking hard about which sector you are going to choose, though.

What sectors should I buy?

While we're on the subject of sectors, you only have to take a quick look at the figures on any financial website to see that there are real and important differences between the sectors. Let's take some examples: in August 1999 the average price/earnings ratio in the electricity sector was 13.5: in the information technology and hardware sector it was 116. This is a huge difference which should modify your strategy a good deal. Sectors that contain blue chips and solid, dependable performers need to be treated completely differently from sectors that involve a large number of start-up companies and smaller outfits.

Sectors also fall in and out of fashion, and these fashion fads can be intimately related. For example, the average relative strength of the households goods and textiles sector was down over 23 per cent in the year up to August 1999. But with the recent hike in property prices, can a recovery in this sector really be far away? And if the boom in the housing market continues, will there be spin-offs for insurance, banking, carpet manufacturers and household retailers shares?

As explained above if you can become something of an expert in one particular sector, then you undoubtedly have a great advantage. Pick your sector carefully, though. You need second sight to even start to understand areas like telecommunications where the game changes so rapidly that even the experts can't keep up. Don't always automatically reject the less popular sectors either. No matter how unfashionable a given sector is, there are always nuggets just lying around to be picked up and banked.

What size companies will I trade in?

It is worth giving lengthy consideration to the size of company that you will trade in. As explained elsewhere, there is a massive correlation between risk and reward. The more reward you seek, the more risk you have to be prepared to take. Generally, the smaller the company the greater the risk. As a rule of thumb, companies appearing in the FTSE-100 have low risk and low rewards attached to them and companies in the Mid-250 have quite low risk and reward. After that, we go down the divisions a bit. Companies in the FTSE Smallcap index can provide pretty high rewards but involve significantly more risk; this increased risk and reward is magnified even more for companies in the FTSE Fledgling index, and once we start to get to AIM and OFEX shares the risks become too high for most sane investors. A simple browse through the share price graphs of a few typical AIM companies is all that it will take to convince you that precipitous falls and extravagant rises in share price are the norm rather than the rule.

At the start of your online trading career, you would be well advised (unless you have a good deal of experience in trading smaller companies through a bank or a broker) to stick to FTSE-100 or FTSE Mid-250 shares. Even here, the recent spate of Internet company hyping has led to some crazy times, and there's much in the argument that (maybe temporarily) it's just as risky to trade on the FTSE-100. In calmer times few shares in the FTSE-100 move more than about 5 per cent in a day.

Another reason to keep away from smaller companies until you feel really confident in what you're doing is the spreads. It's not unusual for a FTSE-100 share whose mid-price is say 1000 to be buyable for 1002 and sellable for 998; a very small spread. On the other hand, an AIM share (whose anonymity I shall grudgingly preserve) recently had a mid-price of 11 but could only be bought for disgraceful 14 and sold for a shameful 8. With spreads like this, once you've paid the stamp duty and the commission, the share has to virtually double in value before you make any real money on the deal. Don't give in to this: no matter how much you fancy the company, if you're offered a spread like this then vote with your feet and seek better value elsewhere

How much will I diversify?

This is another key planning decision. Read virtually any investment book and you'll be told 'buy for the long term', 'don't try to make quick profits' and 'don't put all your eggs in one basket'. Things are apt to get a little more complicated when one buys and sells quite a lot. Of course, we all know that the first two of these sentiments are basically sound. But this doesn't mean that you shouldn't take a quick loss or profit and it also doesn't mean that you should never have some shares in your portfolio that are bought for the short term.

The problem of how much to diversify depends on rather a lot of things. For a start, it depends crucially on how much cash you have. Suppose that you want to start your online trading career with £1000. Does it make sense to use this to buy a portfolio of ten shares? Of course not. You'll be eaten up by commission, spreads and stamp duty and go nowhere fast. With only a grand to play with it's much better to buy just one or two stocks and try to build your capital up. If you feel nervous, then set some stop losses (see below).

The other thing about diversification is that it normally affects your profits as well as your losses. The more shares in your portfolio, the more likely it is that at least *some* of them will be dogs. These poorly performing backsliders will eat into your profits and make sure that you never really make much money. Of course, such diversification is also an insurance policy which should help to ensure that you never lose too much. As you can see, the real effect of diversification is that it decreases the *volatility* of your portfolio. It's up to you to decide how much risk you want to take.

How often will I trade?

Anyone with any sense who writes about buying shares will tell you exactly the same sorts of things that were said just above: short termism is bad: buy for the long term. Compound interest is your friend: not even the best financial expert knows how the markets will move from day to day. We've discussed this already to a certain extent but one thing is crystal clear: unless you have second sight or such outrageous luck that you might as well play the lottery instead you would be a complete and utter fool to base your whole plan around trying to make quick money by buying and selling online.

A Sunday paper recently quoted figures that showed that the average number of trades per year by amateur offline (i.e. via bank or broker) investors was 2, but amateurs who traded online averaged 12 deals per year. Putting aside for the moment the fact that statistics like this are almost impossible to gather in any meaningful way, the difference is striking. An earlier chapter of this book extolled the virtues of doing your trading online, hopefully convincing you how much easier and cheaper it was. How are we to take advantage of this?

We've now got ourselves into the following quandary.

- You should trade and plan long term.
- If you only make a few trades a year then it's not really worth all the trouble of having a real time online broker.

- You're mad to try for short-term profits or to try to predict every click of the market.
- Having the facility to buy and sell online allows one to take advantage of opportunities to make a quick killing.

Don't these all seem to be rather contradictory? Well it may seem that way at first, but there's a perfectly sensible way in which you can have your stock market cake *and* eat it. Suppose that you had £5000 with which to begin your online trading career. Consider the following two start-up portfolios.

- **Portfolio 1**: Buy £1000 each of Glaxo Wellcome, Lloyds TSB, BP Amoco, Vodafone Airtouch and Unilever.
- **Portfolio 2**: Buy £5000 of Systems Integrated Research (an AIM company whose share price has varied between 128 and 4 over the last four years).

Portfolio 1 is as blue as blue chip portfolios come. Gains are practically certain, as are dividends. The money will appreciate slowly and virtually no trading will be required. Portfolio 2 is immensely risky and may rapidly lead to either financial bliss or ruination. If the share starts to dive a quick sell will be required, if there's a big price jump then you'll have to be alert to take advantage of it

My contention is that portfolio 1 is too boring to bother to trade online, while portfolio 2 is just a wild gamble. So why not combine the two?

If you're an amateur then you want to make profit and have some fun as well. So why not do something like not buy the Vodafone Airtouch shares in portfolio 1 and instead buy £500-worth of Systems Integrated Research and £500-worth of SFI (a company that runs lap-dancing joints and clubby-type pubs and which seems to post very fine profit figures every year)? Now you've got an active trading part of your portfolio and a safe part with some diversification and a nice tidy dividend income. Perfect!

Of course, your nice-but-boring blue chips *may* do dramatic things. If one goes up by 20 per cent fairly rapidly, you may decide to take the £200 profit on them and use the money to buy something a little more risky. In any case, a portfolio like this is, in my opinion, much better suited to sensible online trading than something like portfolio 1 or portfolio 2.

What about dividends?

How important are dividends to your strategy? Are you likely to recoil aghast if you come across a company that pays *no dividend at all*? The answer to these questions depends rather on what sort of investor you are. If you are going (as many do) to run an online portfolio which contains a few long-term 'core holdings' (possibly in FTSE-100 companies) and a few more frisky short-term performers then you will probably want to make sure that your core portfolio shares are all good yielders. Most online traders that I know tend to be rather scornful of dividends as they always seem to make up such a small part of one's total incomings, but in my opinion the effects of dividends on the value of one's portfolio are often underestimated. They can build up with surprising rapidity and turn a temporarily bad performer from a sell into a hold. Buy shares that yield well and you'll be pleasantly surprised when you add up your dividend income after a few years.

Whatever you think about dividends, before you make any online share purchase it's always worth finding out when the next dividend payment is due and whether you'll be buying 'ex-div' (i.e. too late to qualify for the next dividend payment) or 'cum-div' (i.e. in time). It's also a worthwhile exercise to spend a little time working out how much you can expect in the way of dividend payments if, say you hold the share for a year.

One thing that you might also bear in mind is that, *according to the mathematical theory of the way that the stock market works* all share prices should take a jump down as a dividend date is crossed. The reason for the italics in the previous sentence is that mathematical models for the markets are all idealisations and may not be fully borne out in practice. In this case, the theory is based on the simple fact that if the share price did not drop then one could make an instantaneous risk-free profit by buying the share just before it went ex-div, collecting the dividend, and then selling it again. The mathematical name for this sort of 'free lunch' is *arbitrage*† and since this is not allowed in most mathematical theories of finance we are forced to conclude that the share price must fall when a dividend is paid.

What risks am I prepared to take?

The oldest law in economics is that risk and reward go hand in hand; 'twas ever thus. The more reward that you expect, the more risk you will have to take. As a general rule, look at the market cap and the volatility (or beta relative) of any company that really interests you. If the former is low and the latter is high, then the rewards are potentially great but so are the risks. Knowing this should materially affect your buying and selling strategies. We've discussed above how diversification in your online portfolio affects the risk and therefore the reward. Sometimes there are chances to buy where the risk is small but the potential rewards are high. If you have developed a never-fail strategy for spotting these opportunities then e-mail me and I promise that I'll never tell anybody else about it. If you haven't, then why not stick to the sort of portfolio recommended above, which combines risky growth shares with solid blue chips?

---

† Two professors of Economics are walking down the street when they simultaneously notice a five pound note lying on the pavement. The professor that does not understand the principle of no arbitrage says 'oh look, a fiver!' and the other one (who does understand arbitrage) replies 'there cannot be a fiver on the pavement, for if there was then by arbitrage somebody else would already have picked it up'. Mathematicians regard this as a very funny joke.

Am I a day trader now?

No. You're not a day trader. You're someone who trades shares online in real time. There's a huge difference between what you're doing and what a day trader does. Since a great deal of people don't seem to really understand what it means to be a day trader, let's point out some of the differences between online and day trading.

For one thing, a day trader typically makes 20–40 trades a day. As you might imagine, it's not possible to do this much buying and selling every day and be a success at a normal job too, so day traders do it for a living and not as a profitable hobby. Day traders also do not normally hold overnight positions: anything that they buy is sold the same day.

There are a number of very big risks in being a day trader. One of the major problems is a simple financial one: if you're making that many trades a day then even then if you're paying low commissions you're going to have to be remarkably successful to show even a modest profit. The basic tactic of a day trader is to try to make non-trivial sums of money from small moves in price. Many day traders therefore trade on margin or buy and sell highly geared derivative products like options and futures (see chapter 9 if you don't know what these are). Operating like this requires you to try to predict every 'click' of the market, and to try to do this day traders make extensive use of 'technical analysis' (or charting, as we would call it in the UK). Unfortunately, 'black magic' might be a more accurate name. Not surprisingly, the majority of day traders make a loss – their strategy yields them virtually the same as they would make if they bought at random, but the dealing charges get them in the end.

There is also a general misconception about how many people really day trade. Although thousands upon thousands of American citizens have online share trading accounts, only a few thousand can really be classed as day traders. The sort of online trading accounts that are available in the UK are not really suitable for day trading either. A special sort of account which is geared to instant and high-volume execution is required and while these are readily available in the US, it's hard to find such services in the UK.

If you are interested in getting involved in day trading, then read some of the books listed in chapter 10. Then decide not to.

Buying

The 'three reasons'

Before we get a bit more advanced, let's start with something that's been in my plan from day 1. It's not infallible, but I am absolutely sure that it's saved me thousands of pounds over the years.

Don't buy anything unless you can give at least three separate reasons for buying it.

By the way, three is an absolute minimum. The more that three looks like it might become five, or ten, or even twenty the happier I get.

There's nothing magical about the reasoning here: shares can go up (and down) for all sorts of reasons, so the more 'positive vibes' you have on your side, the better. It stands to reason, therefore, that when a share has a number of *different* good things going for it, conditions are much more likely to be favourable for you to pounce. So what might these reasons for buying be? The answer to this depends largely on what sort of share is involved. In later chapters much more consideration will be given to what might signal a 'buy', but for the moment let's look briefly at a list of 'buy reasons' that appear in one form or another in many people's online trading plan.

- The company seems to have developed a 'niche' for itself, or has a unique product, or has a stranglehold on the market.

- Some or all of the directors have recently bought shares themselves.

- The company exudes quality: they make good products, are well-run and have a consistent record of turning cheap raw materials into expensive and profitable products.

- Although the company has a good record, seems to be well-run and is making a healthy profit, their shares are undervalued.

- Something is happening in the company's sector as a whole.

- The company has been tipped in the newspapers or by other media coverage.

- Something has just happened that has changed the conditions of the company.

- The dead cat bounce (see below).

As far as my own personal plan is concerned, none of these reasons would be enough *on their own* to buy a share. But when three or more of them happen at the same time, it's generally out with the mouse and on with the e-trading. Let's analyse the components of the 'three reasons' one by one.

Niche markets   Companies that have cornered the market in a particular area are like gold dust. They have a unique advantage which their competitors have to constantly strive to keep up with. Good examples recently have been companies like Trafficmaster who make in-car guidance systems and Glaxo Wellcome who in 1999 released Relenza, then the only currently available influenza treatment of its kind. You might even regard the (now infamous) lastminute.com as a company who are uniquely set up to do what they do. After all, unlike many dot.com companies, at least they have plenty of business and turn a healthy profit. Such companies can often afford to operate on high profit margins. They also often boast a great deal of patents, copyrights and/or general legal advantages.

Directors buying   Directors buy shares for all sorts of reasons, and in all sorts of amounts. But in general they are the people who know what's going on at the company, and so their share-buying actions can mean a lot. In particular, I like to give especial weight to large buys made by Chief Executives or Financial Directors. You might think that this is secret information (after all, when I buy a share who the hell has the right to know except me, my online broker and the tax inspector...?) but legislators insist that all 'director's dealings' are made public for all to see and interpret if they wish (see, for example, the weekend *Financial Times* or **www.hemscott.co.uk** and numerous other websites). Normally, it's even possible to find out *why* directors have bought or sold. You might think that a director would be crazy to divulge why they bought or sold shares (for example, the rather pathetic 'sold to finance divorce' statement) but often directors want to send a specific message to everybody. After all, why should they allow people to think that they've lost confidence in their own company just because the missus was wooed by the milkman? Of course, significant directors' selling is a strong signal to think again before you buy, or, if you own the shares, to consider selling.

A quality company   Quality companies do well year in, year out. They have good staff who are run by good management and they make good profits and turn them into cash. It stands to reason that when you're buying online you should never forget the importance of 'good fundamentals' (which will be discussed more in chapter 5). Don't ever be fooled into thinking that because a quality company has done well in the past the law of averages dictates that it should suddenly start to do badly. Good football teams win week after week precisely because they are good, and it's the same with good companies. On the other hand, just because a company has been a brilliant performer for many years it doesn't mean that the wheels can't come off. Consider the fortunes of major retailers at the end of the 1990s, for example.

Undervalued company   Sometimes companies that really should be doing well don't. Their share price no longer gives a true reflection of how good the company is, the markets down rate them and in spite of their consistently strong performance, the shares slide. In short, the company is undervalued.

The reasons for undervaluation can be complex, but one thing is for sure: fundamentals will win out in the end and good performers will eventually get what they deserve. Undervalued companies are therefore a boon to one's online investment plan and should be snapped up. We'll have more to say later on the subject of how one might recognise an undervalued company.

Of course, there are dangers. Looking back at examples of quality companies that were badly undervalued by the markets, it's hard to find cases where they didn't bounce back eventually. The problem is that word 'eventually'. Companies that are undervalued might become *even more* undervalued before they recover. The tactic of looking for undervalued companies relies heavily on timing, and if there's one thing that it hard to get right as far as the old stocks and shares game is concerned, it's timing.

Sector action   As we have already noted, different sectors behave in different ways. If you take the time and trouble to become acquainted with how sectors behave both within themselves and in comparison with others, then you can't help but notice some interesting features of share price movements that seem to be almost entirely driven by what's happening in a particular sector. For example, surf to your favourite site on a day when the FTSE-100 has made a big move (either up or down) and look at the 'biggest movers' list. Very often you'll find that all the banks and insurance companies have gone down and all the tech stocks have gone up, or vice versa. On another day all the supermarkets will have done well while all the oil companies have lost ground together.

Market makers are fickle beasts who tend to hunt in packs. Once one starts to mark a sector down or up, the other market makers follow like sheep, the institutional investors and pension funds start to buy or sell, and the whole trend is accentuated. You can turn this to your advantage, of course. One simple way of doing this is to wait for a quality company to be 'dragged down' by negative news about another company that's in the same sector. Very often such a move is rapidly followed by a rise back to the status quo. It's also possible to make money by climbing on the back of a particular sort of share when its sector seems to be generally in favour.

Strongly fancied runner   The effects of gossip and publicity should not be underestimated as far as potential share price movements are concerned. The now-legendary Jim Slater first came to the public's attention in the sixties when he wrote a highly popular share-tipping column in a major national newspaper. He tipped 'em, everybody read about 'em, everybody bought 'em, and so of course the price went up! Though to some extent the whole business became a self-fulfilling prophecy, it shouldn't be forgotten that Jim Slater made his reputation in the first place by being an uncannily accurate share tipster.

Appearing in the 'you and your money' section of a Sunday paper as a 'hot tip', being the subject of a sound bite on the six o'clock news ('stock market analysts predict that…') or becoming the star feature of an article in *Investors Chronicle* can all lead to ballooning share prices and worthwhile profits for you to tap into. As you might expect, timing is the major problem. Often you will find that by the time you have digested the news the upward hike in share price has taken place already and you've missed the boat. Without doubt though if you have an online trading account you're in a far better position to take advantage of this sort of media feedback than anyone who stills buys shares the traditional way (i.e. through a bank or a broker).

A change in conditions   Share prices often move when circumstances or conditions alter. It therefore follows that when things are changing for a company, it can be a good time to buy or sell. Let's take a simple example: a company is due to announce its interim results in a few weeks and you suspect that these will be much better than expected. In these circumstances, a buy signal (and therefore one of your 'three reasons') is clearly indicated.

Companies may also make an active decision to change their circumstances. A big brewing concern decides to soft pedal on the beer-making side of its operation and spend more time and money on acquiring hotels, health clubs and resorts (as both Whitbread and Scottish & Newcastle have done, for example). A cigarette mega-manufacturer decides to increase its diversification and accentuate its insurance business (as did BAT). A few years later it decides to do the opposite and de-merge its insurance business (BAT again!). In each case you need to take a view on how the change in circumstances will be received by the public and the markets.

Another obvious way that companies can affect their destiny is by takeover or merger. Share prices can change by large amounts (either up or down) when 'talks' are announced and can swing in the opposite direction when the talks either break down or finally come to a successful conclusion. Whatever happens, there's money to be made by calling it correctly.

The dead cat bounce   Often when a company reveals some bad news (a profit warning, for example, or the loss of a big contract) and its shares plummet suddenly, there are people around who buy straight after the fall, expecting to profit from a reaction against the fall. In its most serious incarnation, this is known as the 'dead cat bounce' (from the traders' maxim that even a dead cat will bounce if you throw it out of a high enough window). A good example of this recently was the computer games company Eidos (producers of the Lara Croft series) who lost 30 per cent of their value in a morning after a profit warning. Sure enough, two days later the price had rebounded by 10 per cent and those who bought immediately after the fall were able to sell quickly for a tidy profit. As a reason for buying it sounds too risky for my taste, but perhaps you want to become an expert in spotting such situations?

Should I buy penny shares?

First, what exactly are penny shares? In prescriptive terms, any share that trades at less than 20p is a penny share. Of course, you could argue that the somewhat arbitrary figure of 20p should be 15p or 25p, but essentially any share whose value is *a great deal* less than a pound qualifies as a penny share. Prudential, Reuters, Boots and British Gas are not penny shares; in fact it's almost impossible to think of a large, established company that is. Very small companies often *are* penny shares, and as you may be aware, very small companies sometimes go belly up in a short time.

'Penny shares offer quick and easy profits' say those who have it in their vested interests that you should buy them, and by jingo, they're right. Unfortunately penny shares also offer you:

- a decent chance of losing absolutely all of your investment;
- the prospect of huge spreads to pay;
- the promise of an illiquid market.

So, for one upside, there are three downsides.

As well as this compelling evidence for generally steering clear of penny shares, it's also worth reflecting that to some extent there's a hidden agenda when a company's share price is very low. The point is that a company doesn't *have to* tolerate such a low share price. One quick share consolidation is all that's required to bring the share price up to around a pound. So why not do it? We conclude that the company *wants* to have shares that not many people buy or sell because of the large spreads and the illiquidity, and this is not exactly a bullish sign.

In summary, there are many reasons for deciding that your plan should disbar lowly penny shares from entry into the exclusive club that is your online portfolio. Whether you actually want to impose a blanket restriction is up to you of course, and will depend very much on your online trading experience. Perhaps the best compromise is to decide that:

- you'll have no dealings with penny shares until you're good and ready for them;

- penny shares will never form a large part of your online portfolio;

- if you're going to succumb to temptation you buy them with your eyes wide open to the risks.

Selling

The sell limit

If you don't already know it, let me tell you something: selling is absolutely, totally and completely the hardest part of online (or any other form of) share trading.

Even though you may have read exactly this statement many times before in books, one tends not to realise exactly what it means until one actually has to face the problem for real. 'But wait', I hear you say. 'Surely the hard part is finding a bargain in the first place?' Quite the opposite. As you'll soon realise, if a share that you have bought is doing well, the tough call to make is to sell at the right time. If a share that you've bought is doing *badly* then it's an even tougher call.

Some methods of locking-in profits to shares that are doing well are explained below, but the simplest strategy is to set your own sell limit and stick to it. For example, suppose you buy £5000 of Marks & Spencer stock at the start of the week at 248p, and by Wednesday they have risen to 260p. Nice! But is it time to realise a quick profit? My instinct (guided by hours of perspicacious research, of course) in these circumstances would be to try to ride the wave of positive vibes and to set a sell limit of say 272p. When the shares reach this, you can sell for a 10 per cent profit: not bad for a week's work. If there is no further movement during the week, then I guess you could hold them a bit longer; after all you wouldn't have bought them if the fundamentals weren't good, now would you? If they go down, then I would hang on as long as the shares didn't hit any stop-loss limit (see below)

The stop-loss

If there is one message that I hope to get across in this book regarding strategy for online trading it is this: you *must* cut your losses. There's no doubt that a failure to cut losses and to stumble on holding shares that are steadily losing their value is the biggest single mistake that most amateur traders (and after all, that's what you and I are) make. One simple way that you can avoid this disaster is by setting what is known as a 'stop-loss' limit. A typical stop-loss might be 15 per cent. This means that if ever the share price drops to 15 per cent below what it was when you bought, you sell.

You might decide to set stop-losses on all of your shares, or only on some. For example, if your e-trade account holds a blue chip and a risky Smallcap share, it might be sensible to set a stop-loss only on the risky asset. To be true to yourself though you have to decide this *when you buy the share*.

Just one more thing: if you set a stop-loss then you *must stick to it*. There can be no backing out, no sudden 'reassessment of the situation' and no 'gut feeling that a rise is just around the corner'. Think hard in the first place about whether or not you want to set a stop-loss, and obey it if you do.

Insurance for star shares

Suppose you're in that lovely position of buying a share that has suddenly taken off. As this inspired purchase of yours soars ever higher into the stratosphere, what do you do about selling? Do you wait until it's doubled in price? Do you leave it until it's a 'three-bagger'? Just what *do* you do? Be clear, there's one thing that you just *can't* do, and that's nothing. The danger of course is that a rapid rise in a share price almost always suggests high volatility, so it only takes a bit of good news to turn into bad news and the share might sink as rapidly as it rose.

Should you ever be lucky enough to be in this situation, there are many ways of dealing with it. The most obvious is to take out a bit of insurance and set a sequence of ever high stop-losses (which in this situation should really be called stop-losing-gains but are normally referred to as 'trailing stop-losses') that rise every time the share goes up. Suppose that you bought at 100p and the share has reached 200p. Then setting a stop-loss at 180p will guarantee you a healthy 80 per cent profit. If the price moves up further to 250p then you readjust the stop-loss to 225p, and so on.

Remember also that in this situation you don't have to sell all of your shares. Why not sell half or two-thirds of them when the price has doubled and leave the others to 'speculate for themselves'? Again, you have guaranteed yourself a fat profit and may still have power to add a lot more.

Problems, problems! These are the sorts of decisions that we'd all like to have to make. Remember though, that it's just as important to optimise your tactics when you're rolling in it as it is when your shares are disappearing south of the border.

Some other barrier is hit

Because knowing the right moment to sell is so hard, many online investors like to make selling the most automatic part of their plan. This makes a lot of sense. We have already discussed the business of setting stop-losses and sell limits, but the sell signal need not always come from the price alone. You could decide, for example, to sell a share if its PER (see chapter 4 for more details) ever hits a certain value. You could also make the decision based solely on relative strength. That way, if your share is decreasing slowly in value against a background of a violently bearish market (and therefore increasing in relative strength) you can use a relative strength sell criterion as a practical alternative to a stop-loss that might be falsely triggered.

Alternatively, as the interim and final reports roll around, you can set a series of hurdles that the share must jump if you are to deign to keep it in the exclusive club that is your online portfolio. There might be a minimum turnover figure that you are willing to accept, or you may decide that the prospective profits for the next year must exceed a certain value if you are to continue rating the share a 'hold'. As usual, the best strategy is probably one that combines many of these features.

The money's needed somewhere else

Needing to release money for something else is as good a reason as any for selling. If the money's needed because your dentist wants to plug five platinum crowns into you or because your teenage son had a party while you were away and his friends trashed the house, then that's unfortunate but you may have to sell all the same. At least the decision has been made for you.

A more difficult scenario arises when a part of your portfolio is performing solidly but unspectacularly, and an 'unmissable opportunity' comes along which you need the money to buy into it. Should you ditch old faithful for a possibly more risky venture or be more circumspect and stick with what you know? Only you can make this decision in the end, but one thing that can help in these circumstances is to carry out a quick 'expected winnings' calculation.

Doing this sum might go something like this: assume that your (boring) share has a current value of 100p and is certain to be worth 105p in six months. Now guess that your possible new buy, currently at 100p, has a one in three chance of falling to 90p and a two in three chance of rising to 120p in six months. Your expected return on the new share is therefore $(1/3) \times 90p + (2/3) \times 120p = 110p$ which is more than your current boring performer.

On the basis of this calculation you should therefore sell your solid performer and buy the new share.

Estimating your expected gain in circumstances like these is obviously fraught with inaccuracy and guesswork. Your forecast of the risks involved and the probabilities that might or might not apply are often values that are plucked more or less out of thin air. This need not matter though. By estimating your expected profit in this way at least you'll be thinking logically about the situation. Making a calculation of this sort may also alert you to downsides that you had not previously considered.

Other Generic Plans

There are as many different sorts of plans as there are shares. Some work for some of the time, some for not so much of the time and some lead inevitably to the workhouse. If you find one that works all the time then please tell me. Particular types of investor back particular types of plan; some other ideas are briefly collected below for your perusal. You may want to become one of these fictional characters or (more likely) adopt just a little piece of their persona.

Mr Divvy

Mr Divvy's plan is simple: each year, he looks only at the top 30 or 50 companies. From these he selects the four or five highest yielding companies and buys their shares. His thinking here is not so much that the dividends will make him a fortune. Rather he relies on the fact that the high yield is indicative of the fact that the company's share price is artificially depressed. In essence, it's therefore a sort of recovery ploy. According to research carried out by the Motley Fool (www.fool.co.uk) and many others, this strategy regularly leads to gains that exceed the normal return of the top 30 or 50 FTSE-100 companies and may be worth a try in some form.

Mrs Peg

Mrs Peg follows the 'Jim Slater plan' (see *Beyond the Zulu Principle*) and attempts to identify 'growth' stocks (which we'll be hearing a great deal more about in chapter 6) by looking at a number of company statistics. The most important of these is the PEG (the prospective P/E ratio divided by the prospective percentage growth rate) and other key indicators are factors like relative strength, cash flow and the company's position in niche markets. On the whole, Mrs Peg does very well, but she knows that she has to be realistic about the fact that her system tends to lead her to buy risky, smaller companies and will occasionally cause her to invest in a big loser.

Master Growth

Master growth has quite a straightforward strategy: he sinks his money into the shares in the FTSE-100 that have performed best over the last six months or a year, holds them for a certain time, then sells. Master Growth used to do quite well with this strategy, but the recent dose of Internet share insanity has left him confused. Does making a profit matter any more? In fact, do your shares do better if you're a company that *never* sell anything and *never* make a profit? Master Growth is unsettled at the present but he hopes that normality in the markets (and therefore in his portfolio) will resume soon.

Ms Dealings

Ms Dealings takes advantage of the fact that all company directors have a legal obligation to let the public know whenever they buy or sell shares in companies that they direct. She therefore buys whenever there is a large or 'significant' purchase by a director or a group of directors; she may also use directors' selling as a sell signal. On the whole, she does quite well, provided she gets her definition of 'significant' correct; occasionally she catches a huge cold as directors buy their own shares in a last desperate attempt to stop their company disappearing down the Swannee.

Mr R-and-D

Mr R-and-D particularly targets companies that spend more than a given amount (5 per cent is about right) of their turnover on research and/or development. Mr R-and-D does quite well, provided he thinks hard about how he can turn his strategy from a rather rude bludgeon into a sharp weapon. For one thing, research and development are no good unless they are ultimately turned into profits; the investment of time and resources like this also normally has to be sustained over long periods (at least a few years) to produce the goods. Mr R-and-D has yet to perfect his strategy, but thinks that it won't be long before he's onto a real winner.

Miss Outperform

Miss Outperform bases her strategy on the research reports that brokers produce for fund managers. These reports usually contain EPS and profit forecasts and an overall recommendation such as 'BUY', 'SELL' or less obvious things like 'BOW' (Buy On Weakness) or 'TPR' (Take Profits). Miss Outperform bases her buying strategy on selecting companies where the brokers' reports have recently contained profit forecast upgrades. Such reports often attract the much sought-after 'OUTP' (Outperform) rating. Miss Outperform especially likes to buy shares that have a consistent record of beating the brokers' estimates. She does quite well, but not all news is good news and if a company tends not to outperform as much as it expected to (if that's not a contradiction in terms) then Miss Outperform has to be prepared for the share price to take an unexpected hit.

Mr Cyclical

Mr Cyclical knows that many shares are 'cyclicals' which have a natural period of their own. This period may or may not coincide with major economic changes or trends. His plan is to identify a few key cyclicals and constantly buy when they're at the bottom of their cycle and sell at the top. When he gets it right, Mr Cyclical does quite well; the problem is that few cyclicals actually have a perfectly predictable cycle. With this strategy, timing is everything and a few months' error can spell disaster.

Professor Benford

Finally, we come to the case of Professor Benford who is undoubtedly mad. He knows that share prices follow 'Benford's law' which says that most numbers start with the digit 1. In case you think that this sounds utterly crazy, perhaps I should explain: roughly speaking, Benford's law applies to things that grow at a rate proportional to their value. What it actually says is that the proportion of numbers beginning with the digit N (where N is 0,1,2,..9) is $\log_{10}(1+1/N)$. Don't worry if you forgot what a logarithm to the base 10 was 30 years ago at school: all you really need to know is that for $N = 1$ this works out at 30 per cent and it follows that at any one time about three out of every ten share prices start with a 1.

Nobody ever believes Benford's law the first time that they hear about it, but if you need convincing then just find an atlas and look at the populations of the

100 largest countries, for example. Almost 30 per cent of them start with a 1. Then try it with the 100 longest rivers in the world, measured in any units you like. It works.

Professor Benford's strategy is therefore very simple: he buys shares whose price begins with the digit 9 on the basis that 'really the price should begin with a 1'. When the 9 turns into a 1, the mad professor sells and takes his profit. I have never seen this off-the-wall share buying strategy discussed before, but (as one might have guessed) it seems to work nine times out of ten. The problem is that the tenth time the 9 turns into a 1 by *reducing* rather than increasing, and that means big losses. Professor Benford makes a few per cent using his plan, but science it ain't.

Make A Plan

This chapter ends as it started. The most important thing that you can do in your online trading career is to decide to make a plan for how you're going to trade, and I make no apology for repeating this fact *yet again*.

Of course, having a plan is one thing and having the wherewithal to put your plan into operation is quite another. What can you tell from the figures? How do you interpret all the company data that's available? And how do you hone and sharpen your plan until it's a potent and profitable weapon? To understand this, it's necessary to really start to come to terms with what makes companies good, what makes companies bad, and how it's possible to predict whether a given share will turn out to be a star performer or not. In short, it's time to have a look at how to carry out the research that will inform your online trading.

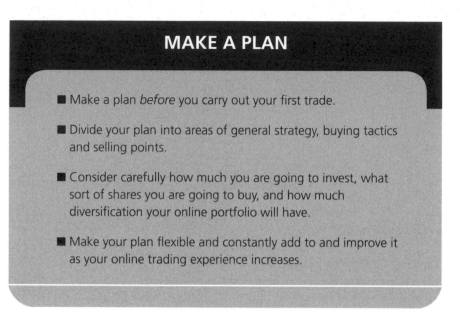

MAKE A PLAN

- Make a plan *before* you carry out your first trade.

- Divide your plan into areas of general strategy, buying tactics and selling points.

- Consider carefully how much you are going to invest, what sort of shares you are going to buy, and how much diversification your online portfolio will have.

- Make your plan flexible and constantly add to and improve it as your online trading experience increases.

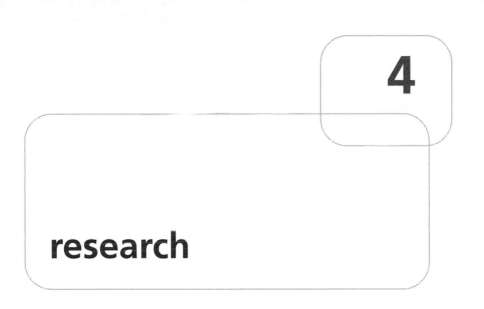

4

research

Research is everything. Forget about luck, second sight and divine intervention: the more you know about every aspect of the companies whose shares you're going to be buying and selling the better you'll trade, and the better you prepare the more money you'll make.

Research is everything. Forget about luck (though you certainly need it), second sight and divine intervention: the more you know about every aspect of the companies whose shares you're going to be buying and selling the better you'll trade, and the better you prepare the more money you'll make. In the final analysis, it's the old story when it comes to Internet share trading: there's no substitute for sweat and toil, and hard work will win the day in the end.

So how do you carry out the research that's required for you to be a winner in the Internet share game? Well one of the great things about Internet trading is that the world wide web is stuffed to the gills and bursting at the seams with exactly the kind of information that you require: it's just a matter of finding it, and using it.

Finding the data that you need is really only a case of identifying suitable websites and visiting them regularly. In the final section of this book you'll find more than enough URL's to satiate your appetite for information. If you're serious about financial surfing, then you'll almost certainly find many more sites that will become invaluable to you. Others will become your trusted friends: you'll visit them day after day, soaking up the facts and figures that they provide.

Using this mass of information is another matter.

- What are you looking for?
- What do all the numbers mean?
- How do you interpret all the data?
- Most importantly, how can you separate the wheat from the chaff and get exactly what you need without suffering from information overload?

Before you can use the available information successfully you have to know what it all means, and the financial glossary at the end of this book tells you just that. It may seem a bit boring at first, but you'll come to know and love these definitions as they give you unique and valuable insights into how your hard-earned cash should be invested.

Fundamentals

Suppose that we agree that we've decided to concentrate on an investment strategy that's based around a long-term view. If this is too boring for you, then let's at least agree that we're not going to let short termism be our sole driving force and that our portfolio is going to contain a mixture of reliable old carthorses and more risky outfits. What should we look for when we inspect a company to see if they're worthy of our money? The answer is simple, fundamentals.

Before defining exactly what we mean by 'fundamentals', let's examine why they're important. The thing is, you see, that the share prices of companies with good fundamentals have a habit of going up. Oh, they don't *always* turn out to be a gold mine, but if they can preserve their fundamentals and keep up their performance then like as not you'll soon be glad that you bought them. Companies with good fundamentals are like batsmen who play straight, never run on a misfield and duck instead of hooking. They may not always make a century or score runs as fast as Ian Botham used to, but come the end of the season they'll be up there near the top of the averages.

The fundamentals to look for

So when we say of a company that 'the fundamentals are good', what exactly do we mean? Well, like everything in the shares merry-go-round, the notion of sound fundamentals means different things to different people. In subsequent chapters we'll distinguish somewhat between what one might look for in a big company and what might be important for a smaller business. Generally, when City traders nod approvingly and mumble 'sound buy, good fundamentals' they are usually approving of things such as the following.

■ A good brand and a competitive edge: Famous, well-advertised brand names with a reputation for quality that everybody buys. Repeat purchase incidence high. Good profit margins and return on capital employed (ROCE). Good investment in research and development.

■ Stable performance: Earnings per share (EPS), turnover and profit that increase year after year. Maybe not by massive amounts, but a steady comforting growth. Dividend yield that increases slowly but steadily and keeps the shareholders happy.

■ Healthy cash flow: Cash flow per share in excess of EPS, solid evidence of an ability to turn profits into hard cash. Cash flow per share larger than capital expenditure per share.

■ Reasonable gearing: A company not up to its eyes in debt who only borrow heavily to finance obviously good new deals.

■ Good management: A stable but ambitious chief executive and board. A firm hand on the tiller.

■ Good financing: Plenty of interest and dividend cover, plus a healthy quick ratio (near to one say).

- Future plans: Evidence of an ability to embrace new technology and to hate the thought of standing still. Aggressive new brand and product development.

You may not know or fully understand what some of the terms used in defining the fundamentals above mean: that's the point of the financial glossary at the end of the book. You may also have other 'fundamentals' of your own that you'd like to add to the list. If you have, excellent.

The dot.com days

Having extolled the virtues of fundamentals, do the markets ever turn their back on what they know is good for them? We all know that sometimes they do, and have periodically been doing so ever since stocks and shares were first traded.

'I can calculate the motions of the heavenly bodies but not the madness of people'. Thus spake Sir Isaac Newton when he was asked to comment on the 'South Sea Bubble', a stock market madness where (as usual) a few made fortunes and thousands lost all that they possessed. The story is a strange one and basically amounts to the fact that in 1720, the South Sea Company, buoyed by extravagant ideas of the riches that could be made from South American property, made the remarkable offer that they would take responsibility for practically the entire national debt. Thousands of companies were rapidly floated, became 'valuable' and then just as quickly went bust when the bubble burst. (Does this sound familiar?)

Amazingly, the South Sea Bubble was not the first example of collective madness sweeping the markets: almost one hundred years earlier the great Dutch bulb scandal of 1637 ('tulipmania'), when tulip bulbs were being

FIG. 4.1. A Hogarth etching and engraving from 1721 entitled 'An Emblematical Print on the South Sea Scene' satirises crowds jumping onto the financial merry-go-round. By permission of the Founders' Library, University of Wales, Lampeter

exchanged for more than the price of a house at one stage led eventually to a disastrous commodities crash which took the markets years to recover from.

So what have tulipmania and the South Sea Bubble got to do with the world wide web? The point of course is that history has a habit of repeating itself from time to time, and this is basically what happened in the last six months of the old millennium and the first three months of the new one when so-called dot.com stocks went through the roof while other companies that boasted perfectly reasonable fundamentals lost half or even more of their value.

Now nobody is denying that the Internet is one of the most important things that ever happened to communications (maybe – or even probably – more important than the printing press). Because of this, some speculation was always likely and some companies who made no money but showed 'promise' were always going to be pumped up to high prices. Unfortunately what happened during those 'dot.com days' showed how uncontrolled optimism (and, it must be said, pure greed) normally leads to ultimate downfall.

All through the winter of 1999/2000 dot.com companies of every shape and size sprang up seemingly from nowhere. Floated without ever having made a profit or even ever having sold anything, prices spiralled up and up as more and more investors jumped on the bandwagon. Companies with only a few hundred employees became so valuable that they displaced the likes of Hanson, Whitbread and Scottish & Newcastle (who employ thousands) from the FTSE-100. Dot.com fever was at a seemingly incurable height, the papers were full every day of lucky investors who had made fortunes in a few weeks, and life seemed rosy.

The only trouble was that even the normally sure-footed venture capitalists and investment trust managers admitted that they had not the faintest clue how to value dot.com stocks. How do you value a company that shows only promise and has never made a penny? The pessimists spoke darkly of 'meltdown', the optimists poured more and more money into tech stocks and those of us with a more boring disposition pottered around buying up some of the undervalued blue chips that had been so humiliatingly marked down.

In retrospect, the turning point came with the launch of the unfortunate lastminute.com, an e-retailer who specialised in last minute holidays and the like and who were co-led by the charismatic Martha Lane-Fox. The flotation was a high-profile one, and the issue was vastly over subscribed. The company then took the extraordinary decision to sell *every* potential investor 35 shares rather than hold a ballot to identify a lucky few who would be given a worthwhile share allocation. Just to make things worse, the distribution of the share certificates was bungled and there were serious failings in the mechanism for returning unspent money to the 190,000 small investors who had tried to buy the stock. Since the flotation price was 380p, being the lucky holder of 35 shares hardly seemed worth getting out of bed for. A few weeks later lastminute shares were down to just above 150p and heading further south.

Worse was to come. On Monday, 3 April 2000 Judge Thomas Penfield Jackson ruled (after a multi-million dollar two year trial) that Microsoft was guilty of a 'predatory' attempt to monopolise the Internet browser market, illegally pressurising computer manufacturers to bundle its browser with their new computers. The technology-heavy NASDAQ index plunged nearly 8 per cent and the next day the whole market tumbled into free-fall. Although the collapse had at one time wiped over a trillion dollars off American stock values, it was followed by a temporary recovery. The jitters could not be calmed however, and when both the DOW and the NASDAQ suffered massive falls on Friday, 14 April the game was well and truly up.

So what do we conclude from this? Just this: unless you are prepared to take a monstrous gamble, stick to companies where the fundamentals are right. Oh sure, the dot.com days were salad days for some. Those that were lucky to choose the right investments at the beginning and sharp enough to know when to sell did well, and jolly good luck to them. For many however (especially the 'first-timers') the experience was much more painful. How would you (or how did you) react to these circumstances? Look at some of the messages that this book has tried to get across: don't base your strategy around buying for instant gain, don't buy what you don't understand, don't risk money that you can't afford to lose and don't try to predict every click of the market. If you had followed even some of these precepts then you'd have survived during the dot.com days. You might even have concluded that the artificial share price depression of a whole host of good companies with basically sound fundamentals created what we old lags know as a *buying opportunity* . . .

Other Sorts Of Research

Numbers and statistics will form the cornerstone of your research effort, but what else can you find out? There are a number of other ways of making your mind up about a company, and you should try to use them all.

Go there

If it's at all possible, go there. This may sound impractical, but it's surprising how much information may be gleaned from a visit to somewhere owned or run by the company that you're interested in. This is especially worth doing in some sectors. For example, take the Leisure and Hotels sector. Consider SFI, a company that runs theme pubs and lap-dancing bars. I went to an SFI pub when I was thinking of buying the shares. The music was loud, the beer came mostly in bottles and the decor was nothing special. Although I only stayed for a quick pint, I noticed that the place was full of young (mostly middle-class) men and women. They were drinking a lot and eating a lot. The atmosphere was brash but good-natured, the bouncers were discreet, and there wasn't a hint of trouble. Most of the customers looked like they went there a lot.

The fact that grandad in the corner (i.e. me) was not enjoying himself very much was irrelevant. I bought the shares and they have done well since.

On the other hand, if you go to a store where the staff are rude, the aisles are deserted, the ceilings are dirty and the prices seem extortionate, then you can't help being put off the shares. A few years ago, Allied Leisure, a company that has interested me for a while, bought some 'Blimpies' sandwich bars to go with their bowling alleys, Burger Kings and nightclubs. I visited their Blimpies outlet in Winchester and hated what I saw. The shop was not exactly spotlessly clean, the staff appeared to be generally hacked off and, most importantly, the customers did not seem to be enjoying their food. Was I pleased when Allied Leisure sold off their Blimpies outlets? You bet. If they hadn't I'd have reduced my holdings like a shot.

So go there. Nose around. Get talking to the staff and other customers. Make a general nuisance of yourself (sometimes this involves being asked to leave. This has happened to me a few times, but I don't mind – it's a sign of good outlet management!). Use your eyes, your ears and your business sense and you'll be amazed what you can learn from a few quick visits.

Ask people

It's surprising what you can pick up about companies by just talking to people. This may not be so useful if you're thinking of buying RTZ (Rio Tinto Zinc), but if it's a company in (for example) retailing, distribution, leisure or media that you're after, then the public's view is important.

A few months ago, after Marks & Spencer had revealed the latest of many pieces of bad news about sales, I was seriously considering them as a recovery stock. Was it really possible that a great British institution such as good old M & S had fallen so far from grace? Was a recovery around the corner? Was the stock a buy at 220p? (Bear in mind, a few months earlier it had been luxuriating in the upper reaches of the FTSE-100 at about 400p.) I set out without delay on a fact-finding mission. One person told me that her mother used to go to the store but now thought that the clothes for women of her age were 'too frumpy'. A work colleague told me that he and his wife had stopped going there ever since they stopped doing maternity dresses, and one of the security guards where I work complained that the portions in the food hall were too small. Now the opinion of three people may not sound like much, but did I buy the shares after that? Not likely.

That was a while ago. Recently, I've heard a colleague at work say that the men's underwear is good, seen their heavy advertising campaign and their new designer label and been to a few fullish stores. They've also got a new slightly risqué underwear designer. Interesting. Maybe it's time for a rethink ...

Sound bites on television, people overheard on the bus, even drunks arguing outside your window on a Friday night can all add to your dossier of information on a company or a sector. Soak it up.

Look at their website

Don't forget to spend a few minutes surfing the website of the company that you're interested in. What, they don't have one? Is it therefore reasonable to assume that maybe they don't have much of a competitive edge, don't use the latest technology and equipment, and are therefore a complete and utter dog as far as buying the shares are concerned? Probably.

FIG. 4.2. Marks & Spencer: will a new website help to revitalise their flagging fortunes?

So you've binned them as a possible share buy and found a company that does have a website. Although it would be foolish to pretend that you can learn *that* much from what's usually on corporate web pages, companies like to boast about things that they do well and you might pick up some valuable information. For example, do they brag on and on about how they're the market leaders in a particularly profitable niche area? Do they witter endlessly about how they have the patents situation for their piece of technology stitched up so tight that none of their competitors have a prayer of even getting into the same league? Some companies' web pages do, and since what they're saying is almost certainly true (it's not generally in the best interests of a corporate web page to lie) you can be sure that they have a competitive edge which could well be one of your 'three reasons for buying'.

It's always worth spending a few minutes surfing a potential buy. Often you won't learn very much of value, but the times when there *is* something interesting can make the cost of a few cheap-rate phone calls seem a bargain.

Read their annual report

Getting your hands on annual reports used to be a problem. No sooner had you sniffed a bargain and decided to investigate further than you realised that the annual report would cost a tenner to buy, and would take a week to arrive in the post. Bad news. You had to be *really* serious about a company to wait so long and spend that money. No more! Yet again, the democratising influence of the www has changed things for ever. It is now much easier to obtain any annual report – what's more, the service is instant and free.

Of course, there's a simple reason for this. Put crudely, if you're an ambitious sort of company, then you want people to buy your shares. If they can read the annual report then they might do just this. So it's an obvious step to put a copy on the web and allow people to download it free. You can do just this at many of the websites described in chapter 10.

What should you look for in the annual report? Your first target should be to see what the chief executive and financial director make of the figures in the report. How do they see the future? Is the chief executive's forecast upbeat? It is cautious? Or is it perhaps so obviously over optimistic that you can largely disregard its contents?

Of course, a great deal of other information may be gleaned from the annual report as well. What is the general tone of the report? How much do the company officers earn and how many share options do they have? Are there expansion plans? Is future debt anticipated?

Read the report carefully and see how it matches up to the other research that you've carried out – it's another string to your bow and you should take advantage of the fact that it's so easy to obtain.

Watch TV

It's surprising really how *little* there is about shares on television. BBC's 'Working Lunch', 'The Money Programme' and the new portfolio series 'Show me the Money' is about all that's currently available on terrestrial television. Going on total airtime alone, do 15 times as many people really play snooker as own shares? The thing about the little information that *does* appear on TV though is the fact that it's being seen by such a large potential audience. This means that maybe it should be given added weight. In summary, although there's certainly some useful information on TV, it looks like you'll be better off spending your time surfing until the television companies get their act together shares-wise.

Track the share

Follow the share for a while. Get an idea of its movements. Are they large or small? Do they tend to come in rapid jumps or little trickles? Does the share tend to move in sympathy or against the FTSE-100 or does the value of the FTSE-100 seem to make no difference? How does the share move relative to its competitors? How many shares in the company are typically sold each day? These are all questions that can help you to get an idea of what sort of animal you're tracking.

Of course, the longer you spend tracking a share the more likely it is that you might realise you've missed a buying opportunity. By the same token however the share might go down and convince you that now really *is* the time to buy. You may also want to track a number of shares simultaneously either by just watching their movements or (more fun) creating a fantasy portfolio that runs alongside your real portfolio. If you're really serious about investing, then track a number of shares and evaluate share buying strategies using ten or more fantasy portfolios. If these ideas seem to work out, then try them for real.

Newsletters and tip sheets

You can be sure that wherever shares and being bought and sold, a ready source of newsletters and tip sheets will never be far away. The general idea is that 'the experts' sell their views to their adoring public in a series of more-or-less dubious throwaway pamphlets. As you will know if you've ever read any of these publications, it's also mandatory to include a section on how well previous tips have worked out (strangely there are few sections on how previous bad tips have bombed) and how the newsletter has outperformed all other similar publications over the last year. So is it worth buying or listening to newsletters and tip sheets?

In general, no. For one thing, although the first few editions invariably come free, they tend to be expensive when you have to pay the full price for them.

Another problem is the sheer variability. Although some newsletters are carefully written by knowledgeable people on the inside of the business, many more are nothing more than a series of wild stabs in the dark. Deciding which is which can be a major problem.

The most persuasive reason for not spending your valuable cash on newsletters and tip sheets though is the fact that so much information is available on the web. A huge amount of raw financial data and massive quantities of general finance sites, e-brokers' information pages and chat rooms and bulletin boards are there for the asking and are all free (apart from the phone call, of course). There are even sites that summarise all the newsletters and tip sheets!

If you can find a good newsletter that you really trust, then it might be an important part of your bargain-chasing weaponry. If you're in doubt though, it's much smarter to ignore all newsletters and tip sheets and put your trust in the net.

Charting

'Charting' is a popular method for predicting the future performance of shares. The basic idea is that, independent of business fundamentals, earnings per share, dividend yield or all of those other annoying numbers that are so hard to interpret, one predicts the future performance of a share by taking a graph of the share price and covering it with dots, crosses and lines. Massively successful (and also occasionally massively unsuccessful) guru Jim Slater was once asked at a Slater Walker AGM for his opinion on the chartists who thought that the company's share price was too high. He replied that his opinion was that most chartists had big overdrafts and ragged raincoats. While I applaud his sentiments, it would be being economical with the truth not to mention that Slater Walker crashed and burned in spectacular style only a few years later.

All the same, charting has become popular. Everybody has their own patent method for drawing yield lines, resistance points, triple bottoms, trigger levels and a hundred other scientific-sounding terms and many brokers (though they might not admit to it) use the services of a chartist. So is there any point in dabbling in what has become a pretty sophisticated business?

In my opinion, not very much. I believe that charting is quasi-science of the most misleading sort and is highly unlikely to answer the key questions that you need to know as an online investor. Before the chartists amongst us (and there are plenty) throw their hands up in horror and send the lynch mob out, let me make clear the reasons for my views.

First, it just does not seem credible that any helpful predictions can be made if the fundamental business statistics of a company are largely ignored. Who cares what the shape of the chart is if one company is in debt up to its eyeballs and has just had its second profit warning of the year?

Second, it's evidently highly dodgy to use charting for anything short term. Anybody who has ever had anything to do with the stock market knows how it fluctuates and how large changes can sometimes occur seemingly for no reason. There is massive evidence that (at least in the short term) share prices move according to what mathematicians call Brownian motion (i.e. randomly) and so charting to try to predict short-term movements in share prices is a hobby akin to betting on which raindrop will reach the bottom of the window first.

'Ah, but charts are for the long term' argue the dyed-in-the-wool chartists. Maybe, but I maintain that most of the time if the charting procedure gets it right, all the chart will tell you is what you could have guessed from using sound business fundamentals anyway. It wouldn't be so bad if the chartists could agree amongst themselves, but ask ten chartists how to interpret a share price graph and most likely you'll get ten different answers. They had better get their stories straight before they try to convince me!

Of course, charting sometimes 'works'. You can even use it for the weather and football. Charting for the weather tells you things like 'snow not likely in July' and 'clear skies in winter bring frost'. Charting in football tells you things like 'teams near the bottom of the premier division don't win many matches' and 'the top teams are more likely to win the F.A. Cup'. Pardon me for being underwhelmed.

Day traders make great use of charts, but then they don't have much choice *but* to. If you're trying to make money on small intra-day movements of the markets then you might as well forget altogether about the business fundamentals of any company whose shares you are buying. Is it any coincidence that most day traders do so badly?

As far as I can see, however, the only circumstances that charting could really be of any practical and valuable help is to help to identify cyclical shares. Plot the correlation between the movements in these companies' share prices against some general economic indicator and you might be able to predict what part of the cycle you are in. As a general tactic though, I reckon that charting stinks.

Just one final word on charting. I recently spent the best part of a whole afternoon looking on the web for a charting-based site which gave complete historical predictions (i.e. every prediction ever made was left on the site so that it could be verified later). I couldn't find a single site like that. Probably they exist and I am just too dumb to find them – any of you online chartists fancy setting me straight?

The Growth Share

What sort of share are we trying to spot? A blue chip that turns in a sound performance every year or a small company that is set for a meteoric rise? The former is relatively easy to find but the latter (often known as *growth shares*) is difficult to identify and even harder to get out of at the right time. Although it's worth introducing the concept now, the analysis of growth shares requires some special tools of the trade which will be discussed in detail in chapter 6.

Organising your Research: a Blueprint

You may understand all the financial terms in isolation, and have followed the FTSE-100 hourly, but how should you put all the information together? How do all the cogs mesh together and turn in harmony to give you a definitive 'buy' or 'sell' message?

Naturally this is the hardest thing of all and if any of us knew how to do it then for sure we'd be millionaires. In real life, all we can do is to try to make sense of all the information in a coherent way and come to a sensible conclusion that's right more often than it's wrong.

To try to help you to perform the difficult task of 'putting it all together', here is a case history of a share buy. This was a real purchase that I actually parted with money for. (All the case studies in this book are real: none are made up.) I talked about the buy with a number of other people who I work with. As far as the markets are concerned we're all amateurs and we know it: by the same token we all happen to be scientists and so we hope that by taking a sensible and dispassionate view we can get at something like the truth. Of course this is a success story: as you might expect, we don't get it right all the time. When you read this example, ask yourself if you'd have reasoned the same way, if there was other information that you'd have included and whether or not you think that the final decision was justified.

CASE STUDY

beer for the boys

It's the middle of March 2000. The share that we're looking at is the brewing company Whitbread. Their current price is 500p and Figure 4.3 shows how the value of the stock has dropped in the last few months. We've been following them for a while and compiling a list of 'upside reasons' and 'downside reasons' for buying the share. We've also included some 'neutral reasons' as these give us the information that they don't provide any information (if you see what I mean). Here's the list:

Upside reasons

■ The current market situation is that dot.com shares have been going through the roof and companies in traditional sectors like banking, retailing, property and brewing have been suffering huge markdowns. Even FTSE-100 companies aren't safe. Whitbread's 1999 maximum price was 1130 and the huge discount that they trade at makes them look like a buying opportunity.

■ The dot.com bubble has reached absurd proportions and there seems to be every sign that it will soon burst. When it does, you can be sure that the investment trusts and big funds will rapidly abandon tech stocks and switch their finances into more traditional areas such as brewing.

■ The company is obviously under careful management. From 1995 to 1999, the pretax profits (in millions of pounds) have been 261, 287, 335, 358 and 366. The brokers forecast profits of 391 and 422 in 2000 and 2001 respectively. Everything seems to point to a nice, well-controlled profit history which does nothing at all to explain the price that the share is currently languishing at.

■ EPS has grown every year since 1995 and is forecast to grow again in 2000 and 2001. This solid performance is another reason why the share's current lowly valuation seems unreasonable.

- ROCE is good (for the sector) at 12.0. This suggests that the company is competitive. Gearing (at 33 per cent) is average for the market and the sector and there seems to be no suggestion of unwise borrowing.
- Sector action looks likely as some of the financial press have been discussing the possible takeover of Kronenburg (probably by competitor Scottish & Newcastle). Historically, the shares seem to move together.

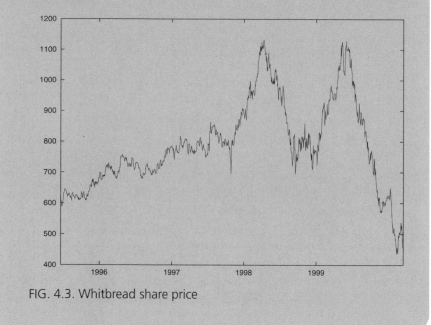

FIG. 4.3. Whitbread share price

- *Investors Chronicle*, the *Sunday Times* (twice) and some of the daily newspapers have recently run high-profile articles on the overvaluation of dot.com companies. All have specifically mentioned the brewing sector as an undervalued area which 'offers investors value in the long term'.

- The shares were recently relegated from the FTSE-100 as a host of largely preposterous dot.com companies were promoted in their place. This has tended to depress the share price even more as the tracker funds have sold and invested in the new FTSE-100 shares. The result looks like an even greater undervaluation of the share.

- The shares yield good dividends which is an advantage if they are treated as a long-term purchase.

Neutral reasons

- There's been no buying or selling of shares by the Directors of any note recently. A few small transactions have taken place but they've been limited to company officials exercising options. No information here.

Downside reasons

- The share has considerable downward momentum. It's a well-established fact that shares with good relative strength tend on average to do better than those with poor relative strength.

- Whitbread has a sort of 'traditional' feel, and this is a fast-changing business. The company profile shows that Whitbread does much more than just brewing: it owns pubs, restaurants, hotels and sports and leisure clubs. But will it be able to meet the challenge of supplying young people with the sort of product that they want to buy or will it go under in a sort of four-ale bar timewarp?
- Competitors Scottish and Newcastle seem to be embarking on a strategy of buying up companies like Kronenburg. Will Whitbread be seen as not being pushy enough by the market makers?

The final recommendation

There are too many upsides not to give it a go. The most worrying part of the deal is the downward momentum that the share price has acquired. Many shares with that sort of price history just keep on dropping. Whitbread seems to be a successful and well-run company though and its boss recently declared himself 'disgusted' with the way that the shares had been marked down. I don't think that that was bravado; I think that he really meant it and foresaw better times ahead.

Furthermore, there is a sort of double reason for buying here. If I'm right and the shares are due for a swift revaluation, then I'll take a quick profit and be away to stalk my next winner. If, on the other hand, things don't start to happen for a while then I'll be quite happy to sit on the shares, take advantage of the reasonably generous dividends and wait for the surely inevitable long-term recovery.

One last thing: in spite of a positive 'buy' recommendation, it's only prudent to be aware of the negative vibes that have surrounded the share for a while. Although (for the reasons given above) I'd be prepared to stand some more short-term falls in the share price, if the downside takes over completely then there could be longer term trouble ahead for the company, and I don't want to be a part of that. So I'll set a stop-loss at 425p and *absolutely definitely* cut my losses and sell if the price ever gets that low.

The result

Bought 1000 WIB on Monday, 20 March 2000 at 503.75p for a total of £5087.64 . By Friday, 24 March (just four days later) the shares had reached 570p and were sold for £5675.05; a healthy profit of £587.41 on the week. The timing was undoubtedly lucky and it was too tempting not to take the quick profit that the shares offered; they would almost certainly have been a good long-term buy as well, however.

There'll be more case studies like this in the next two chapters as we try to address the question of how different sorts of research are more or less appropriate to different sorts of share.

What All The Numbers And Abbreviations Mean

Finally, let's get to the boring bit. As you surf the net looking for the financial information that you need, you'll find that a huge mass of statistics are available even for the smallest and most insignificant companies. So how are EPS, DY, PEG and all the rest of them really defined? More importantly, what do they mean financially and how should they guide your online investing strategy?

The financial glossary at the end of this book defines all the terms and quantities that you're ever likely to need. More importantly, it gives some idea of what each figure means from a tactical and financial point of view. This means that although it's presented as a glossary, it may well be worth reading through it at this point.

The definitions are not completely watertight in that some of the mechanics of working out the figures exactly may be stated a little loosely. This should not matter, however. It's of little use to anybody except accountants to know exactly how the FRS3 accounting standards deal with funds used to kennel the dogs of chief executives when they go on holiday. The important thing is that you understand the basics of what each of the definitions means and how to interpret the numbers that go along with the definitions. Needless to say, others have slightly different interpretations of what exactly the numbers mean. If we all had exactly the same view of what we could tell from a high ROCE or a small PER then investing would be just too easy. Read what others have to say about each of the quantities defined below and let your experience tell you how to construct your own interpretation.

RESEARCH

- Research is everything: the more you do the better your online trading performance will be.

- Learn what all the terms, abbreviations and acronyms mean and how to interpret and use them.

- There are countless ways of researching a possible share purchase or sale: use as many of them as you can.

- In the vast majority of cases, good business fundamentals will win the day in the end.

5

investing in
blue chips

In essence, blue chips are the pillars of the great British stock market: solid, reliable companies that always make a profit, nearly always pay a decent dividend, and have a large market capitalisation.

We've already made some general comments about research and what all the bits of financial data mean in isolation. Now it's time to start putting all of this together and applying it to specific scenarios.

After you've traded online for a while you'll come to realise (if you didn't know already) that when it comes to researching a possible share purchase, not all shares are created equal. Different shares require subtly different tactics in assessing whether or not to part with some of your hard-traded cash. This chapter outlines the sorts of things that you might look for when you are considering buying a blue chip for your portfolio.

What's A Blue Chip?

There seems to be no formal definition of a blue chip, and it's actually quite surprising how different people regard different shares as blue chips. In essence, however blue chips are the pillars of the great British stock market: solid, reliable companies that always make a profit, nearly always pay a decent dividend, and have a large market capitalisation.

It used to be the case that most of the shares in the FTSE-100 (being by definition the 100 largest companies in Britain) were blue chips, but, as we've already discussed, the recent rise of tech stocks has changed this to a certain extent. Perhaps the safest way to define a blue chip now is by how many employees the company has.

However you define them, some blue chips have always been thus and always will be (barring takeovers, mergers, etc.). Companies like BP, ICI, Diageo, Unilever, Prudential, British Gas, Glaxo Wellcome and BT fit into this category.

Should we count Vodafone Airtouch (currently by far the biggest company in Britain) as a blue chip? Its sheer size makes it hard to ignore, but some would argue that its track record is not yet sufficient to allow it into the exclusive blue chip club. Should we count Hanson? A few years ago they would have been in nearly everybody's list of blue chips, but recently they suffered the indignity of being relegated from the FTSE-100. And how about Marks & Spencer? More of them later.

The Post-Internet-Folly Situation

Around the turn of the millennium things all went a bit flaky as far as blue chips were concerned. The full insanity of dot.com madness has been picked apart in other chapters of this book, but as far as many blue chips were concerned the net effect of the dot.com revolution was to lead to widespread share price depression. To illustrate the sort of thing that was happening, let's take the ten largest companies in Britain and compare their share prices at various times based around February 1999 (a date which we somewhat arbitrarily count as being 'before Internet madness').

Table 5.1 shows that in the two years from February 1997 to February 1999, these bluest of blue chips had been behaving exactly as blue chips should, i.e. going up in a nice, healthy, controlled way. The average percentage rise of these ten shares over this period was a whopping 84 per cent, so that on average each stock nearly doubled. In fact, the only company that didn't show a good rise in share price over this period was Shell, which was prey to the variability of oil prices. Cynics will argue that during most of this period the market was in particularly bullish vein, and this is true. But if you calculate

Company	Market Cap (£m)	Feb 1997	Feb 1999	Percentage change
1. BP AMOCO	81,943	340	445	+31
2. Glaxo Wellcome	75,850	1050	2093	+99
3. British Telecom	62,603	440	969	+120
4. SmithKline Beecham	47,384	390	848	+117
5. Unilever	44,121	370	610	+65
6. Lloyds TSB	43,672	506	804	+59
7. HSBC	42,131	527	607	+15
8. Vodafone Airtouch	36,708	60	230	+283
9. Shell	30,750	349	309	−11
10. Zeneca Group	26,407	1700	2780	+64

TABLE 5.1. *Market caps and two-year interval share prices for the top ten blue chips*

Company	Feb 1999	May 2000	Percentage change
BP AMOCO	445	555	+25
Glaxo Wellcome	2093	1946	−7
British Telecom	969	1000	+3
SmithKline Beecham	848	867.5	+2
Unilever	610	376.5	−38
Lloyds TSB	804	616	−23
HSBC	607	711	+17
Vodafone Airtouch	230	267.25	+16
Shell	309	537.75	+74
Zeneca Group	2780	2670	−4

TABLE 5.2. *Recent blue chip share prices*

similar statistics using other periods over the last 20 years then you'll soon see that the general behaviour is the same: it's just the size of the percentage rise that varies.

Now let's consider the situation at the start of May 2000. Table 5.2 shows what happened to (what were) the top ten blue chips (or what we should more accurately call the top ten *old* blue chips) in the time between February 1999 and May 2000. The message is very obvious: blue chips had not nearly such a good time of it while the dot.com revolution held sway. The average rise over this period was only 7 per cent which equates to a very poor year's growth (though still a great deal more than any building society is likely to pay you). Since we took the top ten companies, this behaviour should be mirrored in the value of the FTSE-100. Sure enough, in February 1997 the index stood at 4308 and by February 1999 it had risen to 6175, a rise of 43 per cent. In May 2000 however the FTSE-100 stood at only 6137; pretty much the same as over a year before.

We conclude that there are rather a lot of undervalued blue chips in the market place, and they are likely to take a while to recover. This, dear reader, *is a situation that should be taken advantage of*.

What To Look For In Blue Chips

So you're sitting at your terminal wondering which blue chips should form the core of your online portfolio. For definiteness, let's pluck some figures out of the air. Say that you've decided to invest £10,000 in your online share dealing activities and that you've vowed to spend three chunks of £2000 buying 'safe' shares to put away for long-term growth and dividends and use the remaining

£4000 for other, more speculative purchases. All in all, as we have pointed out before, this sort of diversification seems like an eminently sensible plan.

But which three blue chips should you buy?

On the face of it, you're on fairly safe ground here. As we've seen, blue chips generally enjoy steady upward movement. As we've also seen though, 'generally' does not mean 'always'. How can we pick the blue chips that are likely to give us a nice healthy profit and steer clear of the few perennial poor performers? Of course, there are always a few FTSE-100 shares that outperform all the rest (for example Vodafone Airtouch above) and you'd like to be invested in these if you possibly can be. So what should one look for? The following list is by no means exhaustive and you should carry out your own research to refine and develop it, but to start with it is suggested that you seek a share which possesses as many of the following characteristics as possible:

- a strong brand name;
- good fundamentals;
- a healthy debt position;
- a consistent record of success;
- a competitive edge;
- a share price that's low for no reason.

A strong brand name

For strong, read 'the best'. We want a blue chip to have a high national (and preferably international) profile. We want them to be acknowledged as leaders in their field, and we want them to have a brand name and a series of products that most people have heard of. Where blue chip companies are concerned, being top of the premier league in their own sector rather than just a competent mid-table team who are capable of the occasional shock result is of the utmost importance.

Of course, choosing the *very* best from a set of very good companies is not always easy. For example, if it's the banking sector that we're interested in, how do we choose who to honour with our 'best of brand' medal from say HSBC Holdings, Lloyds TSB, Barclays and Abbey National? One way of breaking the tie is by using some of the filters that are discussed below. The main point is that it's not absolutely crucial. As long as we are picking from the real heavyweights that's all that matters.

Let's make it clear as well that in dismissing all but the biggest and best brand names, we're in no way implying that the rest are necessarily rubbish. For example, where supermarket chains are concerned Sainsbury's clearly falls into the 'great brand name' class. They cater for a particular part of the retailing market, they're known for quality and value and clearly have a very strong brand image. Safeway on the other hand are a different matter. Although everybody's heard of them, compared to Sainsbury's, their brand image has a much lower profile. Notwithstanding this, there's nothing wrong with Safeway as a company. Under other circumstances it might or might not be a good buy. All we're saying is that *when we come to judge the company by blue chip criteria* it evidently fails the brand name test.

Of course, for some businesses it's necessary to delve a little deeper to find how good the brand name is. For example, when you get to the checkout at your local supermarket, how many items in your trolley are likely to have been made by ARM Holdings? Almost certainly none. Come to think of it, can you name *anything* that's made by ARM holdings? If the answer to this question is no, then it's because ARM holdings don't make things to eat, widgets, clothes, beer or cars; they make RISC computer chips. If you did your homework and looked in their annual report, then you'd find that their chips are in a staggering number and variety of computers and other clever machines. For example, two out of every three digital phones sold last year had an ARM chip inside them. They're an established brand name alright.

Good fundamentals

We've already discussed what we mean by 'good fundamentals' and with a blue chip these are especially important. We want to see a record of turnover, profits and EPS increasing year after year in a controlled and sustainable fashion. We want to see evidence of good management, a stable board of directors, a reliable dividend yield, a gently increasing dividend per share, good profit margins and all the rest of it. Above all, we want to see evidence that the snapshot of the company's prosperity that the key financial data has provided us with will still look just as rosy in a year or two's time. Where a blue chip is concerned, good fundamentals are. . . fundamental.

A healthy debt position

Most blue chip companies have debts. The thing that we have to decide is whether or not the debt is a good debt or a bad debt.

Large companies often *choose* to be in debt for a very simple reason: if they can borrow money and make more by using that money than it costs them to pay back the debt, then they're up on the deal. These tactics should be familiar as they are not just used by big companies, but also by ordinary people in their everyday lives. The most obvious example is buying a house. When someone buys a house, there is a sense in which that person can be regarded as a highly geared company.

A mortgage is probably the largest debt that most people will ever undertake, but history has shown that it's usually a good sort of debt to have. Even though the payments may seem ruinous at first, when the debt is finally cleared the property has often grown so much in value (even allowing for intervening inflation) that the whole business can be seen as nothing but a huge success.

Buying a car, on the other hand, is usually a pretty poor debt. Viewed purely as investments, there are very few makes of car that struggle along to even keep up with inflation. Most cars depreciate at an alarming rate and this means that borrowing to buy a car is usually a bad investment.

There are many obvious indicators of whether a blue chip's debt situation is good or bad. One of the most important is the profit margin. If this is around 10 per cent then things are rosy in the garden, for this means that any money that the company has borrowed is yielding more than enough to be regarded as a good investment. If margins are down at around 5 per cent, then the news is not so good. Profits of this sort are unlikely to be able to service a loan effectively and there may be trouble ahead.

How many times will a company's income pay the interest on any loans that it is carrying? As we saw in chapter 4, there is a figure that gives us exactly this information: the interest cover. For blue chips, an interest cover figure above about 7 is enough to give one a nice warm glow inside. A cover of under 4 (especially when combined with low profit margins) would make me distinctly uneasy unless the company had very low or negative gearing.

Another financial indicator that is a great help when assessing debt is ROCE. ROCE does exactly what its definition says: it tells you what return the company makes on the capital that it employs. A high ROCE can therefore effectively cancel out the effects of high borrowing.

Of course, there are sometimes special circumstances that have to be taken into consideration. If a company has decided to buy something big as an investment for the future and has borrowed accordingly then the resultant gearing need not be a problem *provided we judge that the return from the new venture will ultimately be worthwhile*. Often this judgement is hard for a mere toiler like you or me to make, but you should expect to receive considerable assistance from the annual report. If the capital outlay is justified then the chief executive should tell the current and prospective shareholders exactly *why* the company has decided to go down this route, how they plan to cope with the extra debt, and how the company is likely to benefit in the long term. 'Exactly' should really *mean* exactly too. We want hard figures, realistic profit forecasts and an idea of how all this borrowing will affect the company's tax position and all the rest of it. If the predictions aren't satisfactory then shop elsewhere: there are plenty more ships on the blue chip ocean.

Under normal circumstances even if a company's profit margin and interest cover is satisfactory it pays to be wary of highly-geared companies. If there are large loans to repay then any drop in margins may be a harbinger of doom. If you were one of the many who splashed out on the most expensive house that you could afford in the late 1980s or early 1990s only to suffer from the agony of negative equity, you'll appreciate *exactly* what the problem is.

A consistent record of success

A consistent record of success is not *absolutely* essential for a blue chip company, but if you've decided that you want to buy the sort of blue chip that can be placed at the 'bullet-proof' end of your portfolio, then it's just as well if a company enjoys this consistency.

Look back at the company's previous record over the last five or ten years. Have there been unexplained blips in the turnover and profits? In a blue chip, a steadily rising EPS is what we want to see. No sudden peaks or troughs (unless they can be explained away by special circumstances, of course) are allowed: a nice even gradient is all that we're looking for. Of course, there are other measures of consistency as well. Did the dividend yield suddenly drop for a couple of years for no apparent reason? Before you judge this be sure to look at the share price. Take a peek as well at the dividend per share. Happy shareholders make happy market makers and happy market makers tend to mark shares up: one sure way to make the shareholders happy is to increase the dividend per share every year.

Even if all the consistency that one could ask for is present, is it likely to be sustained? One would like a crystal ball, of course, but in the absence of clairvoyant intervention quite a lot can be gleaned from the chief executive's latest public eulogy. How does he or she see future prospects? Are more patents, licences and advances on the way? Is the company aggressively promoting itself, advertising its products and generally looking as though it means business? If you can, compare this year's annual report with the previous years' documents. Are the company doing 'what it does' as well as it possibly can? Does the general direction and management strategy of the company square with last year's promises? Or are there changes at the top and shifts in emphasis that might threaten the consistent performance that's so impressed us up to now?

A competitive edge

We've established that when we buy shares in a blue chip company, we want solid growth and reliable profits. It's a highly competitive world out there though, and to turn in good figures year after year takes effort. Companies that don't constantly try to move aggressively forward normally end up sliding backwards; we want to be convinced that our potential blue chip buy is thrusting forwards and leaving the competition trailing in its wake, rather than complacently resting on its laurels.

One prime indicator of a competitive edge is a dominance in a particular sector of the market. Take the mining sector, for instance. If we look at the August 1999 market capitalisation figures for this sector then we find Rio Tinto in first place with £12,756 million. The second placed company is Billiton with a mere £5,655 million and Lonmin trail in third place with a miniscule £957 million. That's dominance.

Another way of judging a company's competitiveness is by looking at its ROCE and profit margin figures. A ROCE that's higher than average for the sector shows that a company has something special to offer. Good profit margins make an even bolder statement. In effect, the company is pricing its goods or services using a policy that says 'we're the best and we can afford to make you pay for it'.

Naturally, there are other things that can give a company a great competitive edge. One is a guarantee of frequent repeat purchases. Car manufacturers (especially British ones) have never enjoyed this advantage. Many supermarkets do. So do pharmaceutical companies. You get the picture. Another thing that helps is a nice big portfolio of patents, licences and copyrights. Essentially, this means that other companies can use your stuff – as long as they pay through the nose for it. Other worthwhile 'rights' come in the form of business advantages. For example, some electricity companies are legally protected from competition. Don't forget though that they pay a price for this as in return for their protection they are subject to regulation. Don't forget too that franchises are often temporary. If you're thinking of buying shares in Granada Group then whether or not their franchise is up for renewal is of interest to more than just Coronation Street fans.

A share price that's low for no reason

Strictly speaking, of course, there's always a reason why a low share price is low. But is this reason a sensible or a sustainable one? The analysis above of the effect of the dot.com revolution on blue chip share prices is surely evidence enough that share prices can drop for no reasons other than the fact that the market makers are fickle and fashion can drive the markets. A year or two ago there were very few shares whose price was 'low for no reason' (though if you look carefully enough there are always a few around).

As the new millennium gets into its stride, however, it almost seems as though the FTSE-100 consists entirely of shares that are either high for no reason or low for no reason. The observation that there seem to be so few fairly-priced shares around at the moment makes it even more important to steer clear of the overvalued blue chips and latch on to the underpriced ones.

Some Examples

Based on everything that has been discussed above, let's rate a few blue chips. To allow us to rate our ratings, we'll pretend that it's (say) August 1999 and we're raking around the numbers for blue chips to find a possible target for a purchase. To help make a numerical judgement at the end of our deliberations, we'll award marks out of ten for each category. Then if we want to at the end we can make a 'league table'. Here we go then with a few examples.

Example 1: Astrazeneca

There are heaps of people in Europe and the US, and lots of them get sick. This simple fact explains why drug and pharmaceutical companies feature largely in the FTSE-100 list of bluer-than-blue chips, so we'll start by analysing one. Astrazeneca was formed by the merger of Astra and Zeneca at the start of 1999. Mergers are a way of life for pharmaceutical companies and it may not be long before we have to consider the possible financial health or otherwise of Astrazeneca-Glaxo-Wellcome-SmithKline-Beecham-Warner-Lambert-Pfizer.

For the moment though we'll content ourselves with noting that Astrazeneca's main business is making drugs for human and animal consumption, and 'agrochemicals'. As far as *where* they earn their money is concerned, although Astrazeneca are listed on the London Stock Exchange over half of their profits come from the US and just over a quarter stem from sales in continental Europe. Astrazeneca's share price and key financial data (all culled from the web in about 15 minutes) are shown in Figure 5.1 and Table 5.3: the normal convention of showing prospective figures in bold face has been followed. Armed with all this information, let's try to apply the criteria discussed above.

- A strong brand name? Undoubtedly. It's hard to find anybody that doesn't use Astrazeneca products. A wide variety of medicines and drugs that are in everyday use are made by Astrazeneca and as well as common drugs they make all sorts of more leading-edge products. The only downside is that their brand name is slightly less recognisable now than it was when they were just plain old Zeneca. Ah well, that's the price of progress. Definitely **8/10**.

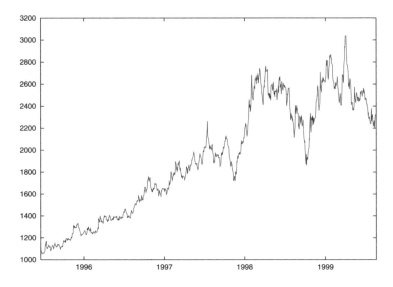

FIG. 5.1. Astrazeneca share price

■ Good fundamentals? Let's take a look. EPS (up by a healthy amount every
year since 1995) is looking stable and satisfactory at the moment. The
company's turnover increased significantly last year and this was reflected in
an increase in pre-tax profits. We also note that the one discernable dip in
turnover (in 1997) was obviously well-managed as profits still rose for that
year. The figures also suggest that everything's under control as far as the
dividend yield and dividend per share are concerned. The management
situation is a little hard to sum up after the merger. The board seems to have

Year	1995	1996	1997	1998	1999	2000
Turnover (£m)	4898	5363	5194	5510		
Pre-tax profit (£m)	878	1023	1094	1136	**2242**	**2832**
ROCE (%)	28	33	36	38		
EPS (p)	62	72	78	84	**97**	**112**
Dividend per share (p)	31	35	39	42	**46**	**54**
Dividend cover	2.0	2.1	2.0	2.0	**2.1**	**2.1**
Capex per share (p)	29	38	46	50		
Cash flow per share (p)	69	81	84	95		

Latest and prospective figures:	
PER	**21.9**
ROCE	37.7%
Profit margin	21.2%
Gearing	16.8%
Dividend yield	**2.19%**
PTBV	10.5
PSR	4.01
PRR	31.2
Quick ratio	0.94
Current ratio	1.34
Interest cover	18.8

TABLE 5.3. *Key financial data for Astrazeneca – August 1999*

remained as stable as possible though and there appear to have been no power struggles or 'policy disagreements'. In summary, the fundamentals seem sound and further growth seems assured: **9/10**.

■ A healthy debt position? Pretty much. Total gearing is just under 17 per cent, but as we will soon see this should be taken care of pretty easily by the company's whopping profit margin. The interest cover is nearly 19, so you can bet that the Astrazeneca board are not exactly lying awake at night worrying about how to pay the company's loans off. That high ROCE also looks good from a debt point of view, and though the general borrowing situation for the company obviously has still to finish sorting itself out after the merger at the beginning of the year, it would be mean not to award Astrazeneca **8/10**.

■ A consistent record of success? The figures speak for themselves. EPS has grown by a healthy amount every year since 1995 (and probably for many years before that; but this is not a history lesson) and so has the pretax profit. The dividend per share could not be more stable, having grown at almost exactly 10 per cent year upon year. The forecasts for the next two years seem to be very good, but we must remember that a merger has taken place. Even so, it's hard to find consistency of this consistency (if you see what we mean) and we can't award less than **9/10**.

■ A competitive edge? With a massive ROCE of 38 per cent and a huge profit margin of 21 per cent, Astrazeneca can't be judged as having anything but a tremendous competitive edge. Quite apart from these stunning figures, they boast a huge range of patents, licences and all sorts of other rights. Their figures shout that they are a market leader; the company that everybody is striving to keep up with. It's an automatic **10/10**.

■ A share price that's low for no reason? That's a little harder to judge. The maximum price in 1999 was 3037 which was attained near the beginning of the year, but the current price is 2323. As we have seen though most things about the company seem to be top-notch. On the face of it therefore the price seems as though it really *is* low for no reason. The only slight problem is that it's a bit hard to assess the effect that the merger between Astra and Zeneca has had on the price. Such things are notoriously hard to judge, and this uncertainty combined with the start of the rise of tech stocks makes us award a cautious **7/10**.

In total we therefore award Astrazeneca **51/60**. Our analysis of the company as a blue chip has taken only a few short pages, and before parting with a substantial sum of money you might well want to process the data in Table 5.3 in a great deal more detail. Even the above somewhat rapid analysis shows, however, that as a blue chip Astrazeneca represented a pretty good buy in August 1999. Sure enough, by May 2000 the price had recovered to 2800.

Example 2: Marks & Spencer

Marks & Spencer have already been mentioned a few times in this book, and in a way it's a pity that they've become the classic 'fallen angel' of the FTSE-100. So what are things like in August 1999? To find out, let's fire up our trusty browser and surf for the information that we need. The key financial data is in Table 5.4 and the share price in Figure 5.2: all we have to do now is to try and make sense of it.

Again, let's start off with some general facts about the company: Marks & Spencer make 96 per cent of their turnover from retailing and the other 4 per cent from providing financial services. Interestingly, 77 per cent of their profit comes from the former and 23 per cent from the latter, which is a good indication of how much tougher it is to make money in retailing rather than money-lending. As far as M & S's global geography is concerned, 97 per cent of their profit is

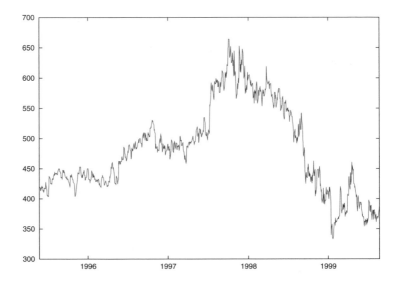

FIG. 5.2. Marks & Spencer share price

made in the UK and 3 per cent in the US. Their operations in the rest of Europe make a *loss* of 16 per cent, and their Far-East businesses lose about 1 per cent. We conclude that any attempts that the company has made to become a global player have certainly not yet succeeded.

■ A strong brand name? Whatever criticisms you have of Marks & Spencer, you can't knock their brand name. It's known the world over and has been carefully nurtured and developed to suggest an attractive mixture of quality, good value and general reliability. If you think carefully about it, the development of the M & S brand image has been something of a

Year	1995	1996	1997	1998	1999	**2000**
Turnover (£m)	6807	7234	7842	8243	8224	
Pre-tax profit (£m)	930	995	1104	1105	628	**689**
ROCE (%)	21	20	20	18	10	
EPS (p)	23	24	27	27	16	**17**
Dividend per share (p)	10.3	11.4	13.0	14.3	14.4	**14.5**
Dividend cover	2.2	2.1	2.1	1.9	1.1	**1.2**
Capex per share (p)	11	8	8	15	11	
Cash flow per share (p)	24	20	23	24	5	

Latest and prospective figures:	
PER	**21.6**
ROCE	9.55%
Profit margin	7.3%
Gearing	26.5%
Dividend yield	**3.82%**
PTBV	2.24
PSR	1.33
Quick ratio	1.40
Current ratio	1.65

TABLE 5.4. *Key financial data for Marks & Spencer – August 1999*

modern-day miracle. We've all heard statistics of the '80 per cent of the Wembley crowd at the cup final are wearing something made by Marks & Spencer' variety but somehow the company has managed to position itself so that nobody interprets this as a sign that goods from Marks & Spencer's are 'common'. However you slice it, the brand name is a winner. Being pessimistic by nature though, we'll take off a mark in acknowledgement of the fact that their brand name might not mean so much to the teenagers and young adults of today. The final score for brand name is thus **9/10**.

■ Good fundamentals? As far as management and the general running of the company has been concerned, recent months have not been good for stability. Some high-profile changes in key company personnel have not exactly left the impression that the board are happy. The company's turnover, profit and EPS statistics (which will be discussed further below) also leave a lot to be desired. Although the dividend per share has just about managed to keep increasing, can it be long before Marks & Spencer actually have to *cut* their dividend? We conclude that in spite of a few healthy-looking items of data our score for fundamentals cannot reasonably be more than **3/10**.

■ A healthy debt position? The company's current gearing is 26.5 per cent which is about average for both the market and the sector. This reasonable level of gearing means that servicing debts will not be one of Marks & Spencer's main problems, and though the profit margin is merely average it's hard to conclude that Marks & Spencer have been profligate in their borrowing. As far as simple cash flow is concerned, in 1999 the capital expenditure per share was more than the cash flow per share (probably for the first time ever in the company's history). However, the healthy state of the quick ratio and the current ratio provide evidence that the overall debt situation is well in hand. We conclude that if there *are* problems at the house of St Michael, then they're not debt-driven and accordingly we award the company **8/10**.

■ A consistent record of success? Herein lies most of the trouble. Look at the share price in Figure 5.2 and compare this with the values of EPS shown in Table 5.4. Before 1997, both of these quantities had been growing in exactly the way that they should for a blue chip. In 1998, however, you can see a clear fall in the rate at which EPS rose, and this was followed by a disastrous fall in EPS in 1999 from 27.2 to 15.8. Were there exceptional circumstances to cause this? Looking at the pre-tax profit figures we find that the company made £930 million in 1995, £995 million in 1996, £1104 million in 1997, £1105 million in 1998 but just £628 million in 1999. The prospective figures for 2000 and 2001 look a bit better, but it's clear that the days of profits in the thousand million pound area have certainly vanished for a while. Do we take any comfort from the fact that the dividend per share has been maintained during these recent hard times? Not much. The least they could do was to keep the shareholders happy. Consistency? The past counts for nothing, the present and the future are all-important, and so we can only award poor old M & S **0/10**.

■ A competitive edge? Strive forward and ye shall succeed. Stagnate and ye shall wither on the vine. So are M & S strivers or witherers? In the 'general retailers' sector M & S are the largest company in terms of market capitalisation (£10,955 million) but there is plenty of competition. Kingfisher, Boots, Great Universal Stores and Dixons all have market caps of over £5,559 million. Marks & Spencer's position is thus hardly dominant. Good ROCE and profit margin figures could confirm competitiveness, but here we are in for a disappointment. ROCE is 9 per cent which is below average for the market in general and *well below* average for the sector. Although margins at 7.20 per cent are average, they're nothing to write home about (Kingfisher, Boots and GUS all do better). A further worry is the way that Marks & Spencer have been trying to take things forward. There have been constant (and public) wrangles with their suppliers, and continual press stories about firms that have been making things for M & S for years being dispensed with. Worse, the general feedback that one gets from the media and the public in general is that the company name, far from being exciting and forward-looking, is starting to exude an air of dowdiness and general malaise. Finally (as we noted earlier) the company's European and Far East expansion initiatives look like loss-leaders at best and complete failure at worst. This worrying combination of statistics and general impressions means that our 'competitiveness' mark has to be as low as **2/10**.

■ A share price that's low for no reason? No. We have to be quite clear here that there is no case at all for regarding the share price as being low 'for no reason'. The fundamentals have been disappointing, the market makers have noticed, and the stocks have been marked down accordingly. The only thing that we might bear in mind is that, in spite of everything, Marks & Spencer do still make a large profit, and it's possible that the markets have slightly overdone their pessimism. Accordingly, for this category we award **2/10**.

In total we therefore award Marks & Spencer **24/60**. This suggests that as far as blue chips are concerned, there is likely to be better value around elsewhere. In the final analysis the company has fallen from grace and lost its formerly bullet-proof blue chip status. In fact, by May 2000 the share price was hovering around 250p; not a disaster but not a blue chip type of performance either.

Hindsight is a wonderful thing

Of course, you're not impressed. You know perfectly well that both of the previous analyses could have been written in May 2000. The real skill, you'll cry, is to be able to predict the *future*, not just to compare share prices now with those a while ago and then waffle on about how the company data made the share's performance 'inevitable'. Fair enough. Let me point out, however, that actually both of these analyses *were* made in August 1999. We have to be realistic though. Even blue chips are fickle beasts, and nobody can expect to get it right every time. What you *can* do is to sway the odds in your favour, and what I've been trying to formulate is the basis of a plan for doing just that.

Note as well that the research needed for the examples above was not exactly of the Nobel-prize winning variety. In fact an hour or two's concentrated surfing around one's favourite financial data sites should have been more than enough to produce each recommendation. The great South African golfer Gary Player used to observe wryly that 'the more I practise the luckier I get' and of course the same applies to doing research into possible blue chip purchases. In time you should develop your own *modus operandi* where the small number of financial indicators described above are but a few airgun pellets in your awesome arsenal.

The Future For Blue Chips

As I've tried to indicate, until fairly recently, picking blue chips was rather easier than it is now. By the same token, most blue chips had the sort of low volatility that one expected of well-behaved core businesses rather than the bungee-jumping tendencies that some large company's shares seem to have exhibited recently and so opportunities for quick gains were rare. So if conditions have changed somehow, then what does this all mean for the blue chips in your portfolio?

Essentially, there are two prevailing views. One says that yes, the markets became afflicted with a bout of temporary madness, yes, things were pretty dodgy while this was going on but no, it won't continue now that the dot.coms have met their Waterloo. In other words, normal service will be resumed as soon as possible. There is a second view, however, and it seems to be gaining in acceptance. This is the thesis that things have really changed for good. Some brokers and banks are already advising that traditional 'buy and sit tight' tactics may no longer be appropriate and investors should hold blue chips for months rather than years. This would represent a sea change in blue chip strategy which would affect pension funds, trackers and hedge funds as well as amateur investors.

It's hard to predict the future for blue chips. Although the markets may remain volatile for a while, it should not be forgotten that there have been many previous occasions over the years when things were supposed to 'change for ever' but didn't. Of course, if a permanent change in conditions for blue chips *does* take place, then one thing is for sure: if you're an experienced e-trader then you'll be in an ideal position to take advantage of the new order of things.

Whatever happens, we'll still be looking for stability and reliability from a blue chip. However the markets behave in the future there will always be big companies with good products and good management whose profits don't allow their shares to do anything *but* grow as a blue chip should. Using the financial indicators and methodology described above, you should have a better than even chance of picking blue chips that will form the profitable core of your online portfolio.

BLUE CHIPS

- Blue chips are the safest sort of shares that you can buy; they form the core of many successful online portfolios.

- Fundamentals, brand name quality and consistent success are all important for blue chip shares.

- Many blue chips suffered big price falls in the dot.com revolution and are likely to be undervalued for a while.

- Blue chips have been uncharacteristically volatile since the end of the old millennium. It remains to be seen whether or not this behaviour will continue.

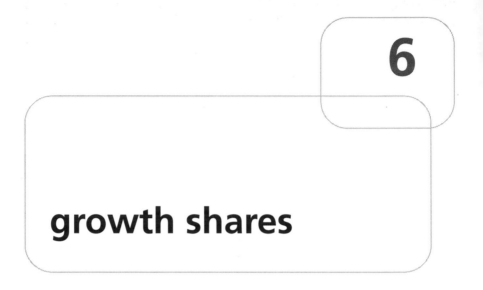

6

growth shares

Growth shares can yield large and rapid profits – but they can also drop like a stone in value if something goes wrong.

So you've gained a bit of experience with those old blue chips from the FTSE-100 and a few solid performers from the FTSE Mid-250. You've not done badly, but you've never had a lot of *excitement* from your shares. You want at least part of your online portfolio to consist of shares that may *really* halve or double fairly quickly. You don't think that the old ticker could stand the high-rolling investment thrills and spills of options, warrants or futures but you want to, ... well, *live* a little. Fine. We have the perfect recipe for you. What you need is to try to get your money on a few *growth shares*.

Growth shares are the sort of shares that everybody wants to buy, but only the lucky few manage to consistently identify. Figure 6.1 shows the share price graph of Black's Leisure, a classic growth share. What are the main features of growth shares? Put bluntly, they grow. Fast. A growth share ploughs its share price furrow ever upwards, underpinned by spiralling turnover, ever-increasing profits and wildly enthusiastic customers who are falling over themselves to order the company's products in ever-increasing quantities.

As Jim Slater sagely observes in his book *The Zulu Principle*, 'elephants don't gallop', and so most growth stocks tend to be from the smaller indices, have rather low dividend yields and rather high P/E ratios – growth is the name of the game and something has to be sacrificed so that the business can expand. Growth shares may also have frequent rights issues for the same reason: money for new acquisitions is constantly needed.

The picture that we are building up of a growth share includes increases in EPS year after year, fast-rising turnover and profits and lots of other good things as well. Most of the time these lead to a share price that goes through the roof. There's just one *teeny* problem though, which is that sadly growth shares can also drop like a stone in value if something goes wrong. In case you're still wondering about Figure 6.1, Black's Leisure were a growth share between 1995 and May 1997, after which they ... weren't.

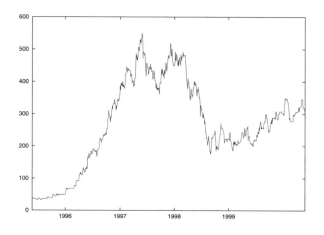

FIG. 6.1. Share price for Black's Leisure, a typical growth share

And herein lies the two great challenges in growth shares: spot them at the right time and sell them at the right time. Let's deal with each of these two difficult feats one at a time.

Spotting A Growth Share

This is primarily a book about online trading and not about growth shares, so straight away I should make it clear that if you're interested in growth shares you should read *The Zulu Principle* and/or *Beyond the Zulu Principle* by Jim Slater. Both of these books concentrate almost exclusively on how to spot growth shares. They are excellently written and they should be your first port of call if growth shares are your thing.

Just to give you an idea of the sort of things that you should be looking for in growth shares however, let's briefly round up some of the received wisdom that has helped many a growth stock follower.

The PEG – part 1

Probably the most important measure which might identify a growth share is the PEG (Price/Earnings Growth ratio). This is worked out by simply dividing the prospective P/E ratio by the prospective growth rate (in per cent). The PEG gives an instant idea of how a company is growing and how that growth has been reflected in its price. Although the general idea of a PEG-type measure has been around for many years, it was really Jim Slater's methodology and research that brought the PEG to prominence. Many subsequent tests have confirmed its value in helping to identify growth shares.

It is important to note that the PEG is worked out using *prospective* values. Put more cynically, it is worked out using the guesses of the brokers for the year(s) ahead. Such 'brokers' consensuses' are actually normally far more than guesses, however. They are based on known details of future order books, knowledge of contracts that have already been negotiated and a great deal of other inside information. As a result they are often (but not always) very accurate.

The element of 'looking into the future' is crucial as far as the PEG is concerned, and this is another reason why the Internet has revolutionised things. Up to few years ago, it was very hard to put your fingers on a large number of brokers' consensus figures without either paying through the nose for them or 'knowing the right people'. That's all changed now and they are available via the world wide web to *everybody*.

Should we work out a PEG for every company? Opinions on this are divided, but many refuse to award a coveted PEG to a company unless it has achieved some sort of sustained good performance over the last few years. This is generally a very sensible ploy as it prevents us from wasting our time getting excited about companies that have extremely low PEGs for the sole reason that their share price is close to zero because they are about to go bust. A typical strategy is only to allow a company to have a PEG if say the previous three or four years have all seen increases in EPS. Other pundits also exclude certain sectors from PEG calculations as there is compelling evidence that PEG values mean far less for cyclical companies.

What does the PEG of a company really mean? Well if we insist on recent sustained growth as explained above then for one thing the very existence of a PEG is a confirmation of past consistent market-beating performance. If the PEG is also low (for example, in the range 0.5–1.0) then this indicates characteristics of both safety and aggressiveness. The safety comes from the fact that shares with low PEG values tend to be able to absorb small pieces of bad news without dropping much in price. The aggression comes from the fact that if PER increases then this is likely to be reflected in an increase in share price.

OK, so we're all agreed that as far as growth shares are concerned having a nice low PEG is a great sign. But is that all there is to it? Predictably, the answer is no. If it was that easy then we'd all be abroad sunning ourselves and statues of Jim Slater would beam down at us from plinths in every park and town hall. Although the PEG is a truly multi-dimensional measure of a company's potential as a growth share, by itself it is nowhere nearly enough to guarantee good times ahead. To give ourselves a better than even chance of finding a good growth share we therefore have to dig a little deeper.

Let's begin by examining a few examples of low-PEG companies that may or may not have turned out to be growth shares. Somewhat arbitrarily, let's choose to look at the five companies that had the lowest PEGs in February 1999 on each of the smaller indices and compare their prices six months later. The figures are presented in Table 6.1 where, for ease, we've excluded companies that were taken over, merged, or had share consolidations, splits or scrip issues in this period.

Some things are immediately obvious from Table 6.1:

- the smaller the index the company is in, the smaller the PEGs generally are;
- some low PEG shares did spectacularly well (Cammell Laird, Luminar, Northern Leisure, Springwood, Watermark);
- a few low PEG shares turned out to be dogs of the most flea-ridden kind (MSB Intl, Shalibane);
- overall, most low PEG shares did pretty well.

Our conclusion (which has been reached by others on many previous occasions) is that the fact that a share has a low PEG is often an indicator of good future growth prospects, but can also be a warning of an impending grisly fate. The question is, how can we refine our searching methods to sieve out the poor prospects with low PEGs and leave only the future growth stars?

Before we consider this, one final point is worth making. You may well have spotted that if you decided to choose your portfolio based *only* on low PEG values, then with the above example you'd have done very well. If you'd covered 15 of these shares equally say, then in spite of the few backsliders in the list you'd have made a pretty profit. Is it just that the month that we chose was special? Not really. It actually turns out that *over the last few years* the strategy of blindly backing

(Smallcap)	PEG	Price Feb 99	Price Aug 99	Percentage change
Photobition Group	0.31	234	224	−4
Cammell Laird	0.33	720	933	+30
Luminar	0.34	680	938	+38
Northern Leisure	0.35	125	177	+42
SFI Group	0.46	192	243	+27
(Fledgling)				
Springwood	0.19	74	162	+119
MSB Intl	0.24	264	162	−39
RCO Holdings	0.25	179	248	+39
Watermark Gp	0.26	33.5	53.5	+60
Emess	0.26	19	23.8	+25
(AIM)				
Shalibane	0.13	134	48.5	−64
Deep-Sea Leisure	0.13	240	255	+6
Kingfisher Leisure	0.13	138	166	+20
Inter Link Foods	0.15	115	140	+22
Jardiniere Inters	0.17	35.3	51	+44

TABLE 6.1. *Lowest PEG companies for FTSE Smallcap, FTSE Fledgling and AIM indices (February 1999)*

low PEG shares would have done very well for you. The fallacy of this 'perfect system' is that over the last few years the markets have enjoyed a monster bull run. There is a serious danger that the tactics of buying low PEG shares by rote will do much worse in a neutral or bear market.

The PEG – part 2

So a low PEG is good, but is not in itself enough to guarantee the sort of meteoric share price rises that we are looking for. That much we know. The obvious strategy now is therefore to add some more refinement to our method. What we need to do is to find some way of weeding out the reprobates like Shalibane and MSB International. How one does this is pretty much a matter of taste. If you think hard about growth shares and take research seriously then the chances are that you'll develop your own tests and methodology. You'll also no doubt want to experiment with (preferably rather a lot of) dummy portfolios to see whether your own personal system works and how it can be improved.

What will your personal system be based around? To try to get the basis of a methodology together, let's briefly consider how we might sharpen our PEG weapon. Improvements to the system might include asking yourself the following questions about your favourite low-PEG share before you splash out.

Does the share price have some upward momentum?

The perfect sort of growth share to buy is one in a company that's on a roll. If we're going to be scientific about it though, then we have to be a little careful about how exactly we define 'upward momentum'. It would be unfair to penalise a share for a small fall in price if the FTSE-100 was dropping through the floor. In fact, under these circumstances we might conclude that our potential growth share was actually doing rather well. What we need to measure is *relative strength*. This shows how the share has performed compared to the market at large. It may also be helpful on occasions to measure a share's strength relative to its own sector.

For most bona-fide growth shares the relative strength should be nicely positive for the previous month, more nicely positive for the previous three or six month period and extra-nicely positive for the previous year. Exhaustive studies have been carried out to assess the importance of good relative strength in the selection of growth shares, and these appear to show that (in contrast to blue chip shares, where the recent share price history tends to be less important) relative strength is a key factor in separating real growth shares from mere charlatans that happen to have low PEGs. Of course, shares with negative momentum *may* increase in value as well. It's just that those with a good recent record tend to more often.

What's the company's cash situation?

Cash flow is crucial to small companies as it's necessary to service their loans, pay dividends and fund future expansion. Without cash, a small company's life blood runs dry and ruin can often follow. To try to get a handle on a company's general financial health, we first need to know if the cash flow per share is more than the capital expenditure per share. If it is, that's a good sign as it means that profits are being converted into hard cash and not frittered away. When the high-profile online fashion shop boo.com went bust in May 2000, their average sales were £80,000 a week and their average expenses were £700,000 per week. We sort of want our prospective growth company to behave like the *opposite* of this cash flow nightmare.

As well as the capital expenditure per share, how does the cash flow per share compare with earnings? If cash flow per share exceeds EPS then obviously things are in good shape. The business has plenty of spare cash to pay dividends with and set all sorts of exciting new plans in motion; just the sort of thing that we want to see in a growth company.

Finally, what's the company's price-to-cash flow ratio? Obviously if it's low then that can mean one of two things: either the price of the share is unusually low, or the company has a healthy cash flow situation. Although it's dangerous to use a company's PCF ratio in isolation, a low PCF can often provide confirmation of a hale and hearty cash flow situation.

Although a prospective growth share's PEG may be low, is the PER of the share also reasonably low?

If not, then there can be trouble ahead. To understand the problem, consider the AIM company NSB Retail Systems. In August 1999 their PEG was a nice low 0.57 but their PER was 29.1. What growth rate does this correspond to? A simple calculation shows that (since PEG = PER divided by prospective percentage growth rate) the growth rate for NSB retail systems works out at 52 per cent. Another few years of this sort of growth, and Microsoft had better start planning how to resist the inevitable hostile takeover bid!

The point of course is that such huge growth rates cannot possibly be sustained for very long. This means that growth shares with PERs above about 15 have a potentially fatal weakness, for when the markets begin to drop or growth begins to slacken the share price could be left vulnerable.

What's the debt situation like?

In many cases growth companies need to borrow substantially to keep growing, but if their net gearing is much over about 40–60 per cent then some explanation is required. After all, if the gearing is very high then some of the profits will have to be used to pay the interest off (from which we conclude that a large profit margin is normally essential for a heavily-geared company). Highly-geared companies are obviously also at the mercy of interest rate rises. Of course, there's gearing and gearing. If you borrow £50,000 to buy a house over 30 years then you're heavily geared – but in a controllable, long-term fashion. On the other hand, if the £50,000 is to fund an evening at the local casino and must be paid back the following week, then there is cause for concern. For this reason, you should make some attempt to discover something about the time scale of a heavily-geared company's debts. Of course, negative gearing (i.e. the company are *owed* money) is an altogether good thing. It's hard though for most growth companies to put themselves in this enviable position. Most smaller companies who want to really go places have to borrow to fund their dreams.

It's hard to overstate the importance of the debt and cash flow situation for growth companies. Their finances are often balanced on something of a knife edge and a combination of excessive gearing and poor cash flow can bring a business to its knees with alarming (and expensive, if they happen to be part of your online portfolio) rapidity. It follows that with growth companies you ought to pay particular attention to what kind of safety nets are in place to protect your investment if things should start to go pear-shaped. For example, are the interest cover, quick ratio and current ratio nice and healthy or will a mere whiff of bad news bring the whole house of cards tumbling down?

Has there been any significant Directors' selling?

If there has, then the powers that be may know that the company is set for harder times and be taking their profits now. On the other hand, if there is notable Directors' buying, this is obviously a very bullish sign.

Directors' dealings are a great deal more important for growth stocks than for blue chips. No single person is likely to own a significant fraction of a heavyweight company like insurers Royal & Sun Alliance (last time I looked, the largest director's holding was a mere 60,000 out of 1423 million shares). For a small company, however, things may be very different; for example, over two-thirds of the shares in finance company Park Group (market cap £162 million) are owned by the chairman. It therefore follows that *any* directors' dealings in small companies are worth analysing.

Note also that if you're involved in the highly risky business of looking for growth shares in the tech stocks sector, then how the directors handle their shares may be of an altogether more crucial importance. Many recent tech company flotations included provisos that the directors could not sell shares for a certain period of time after flotation. If they sell as soon as this time limit expires, the market can become flooded with shares and the price may take the down elevator with calamitous rapidity. Often the key date is the anniversary of the flotation.

If this is the deal then *you'd better know about it*.

The PEG is based on estimates for the future

So have these changed at all recently? For example, have recent brokers' estimates been more or less enthusiastic about the company? Have they revised their estimates of future profits, EPS and dividend payments up or down? Or have the brokers reckoned that they're still pretty accurate and left their estimates largely unchanged?

Changes in broker forecasts can be very hard to interpret. They may be due to nothing more complicated than the fact that the brokers guessed wrong the first time around. On the other hand, changes in one- and three-month brokers' estimates can indicate a worrying trend that underlying growth is slowing down, or be a sign that a share is about to take off. It often pays to keep track of forecast changes as they occur and to think seriously about them if either the changes involve large amounts or a particular positive or negative trend is repeated from month to month. Of course, if the broker's final recommendation changes as well, then rapid action may be required. For some growth shares, nothing can be more damaging than being downgraded by a major broker from a 'BUY' to a mere 'HOLD'.

Why is the company a good growth prospect?

Are they just well-run or is there something more to it? In particular, would they win a 'best of breed' award at Crufts'? Two sure-fire signs of that little bit of something special are high margins relative to the sector and a high ROCE; often these two desirable features go together. Just as for blue chips, high margins show that a company has such a good product to offer that it feels that it cannot be undercut and can afford to charge well for its services. A high ROCE shows that a company can keep on and on ploughing large slices of its profits back into the business. This in turn keeps growth rolling along. By the same token, a decline in margins and/or ROCE can be a sign that a company is losing its edge.

A company may be competitive at the moment, but what expansion plans are in the pipeline? How aggressive is their acquisitions policy? What is the company doing to make sure that its competitors are kept trailing in last position? If an average of 11 new outlets have been opened in each of the last three years but no new stores are planned for next year, then why? Is there a good reason or is stagnation setting in? Have the company overreached themselves or are they merely embarking on a much-needed period of consolidation? The answers to all of these questions can be found on the web, and should give you a detailed picture of whether or not you're planning to buy an ultra-competitive high-flyer or a meandering dog.

What was revealed at the last interim or final report?

Has the company merely been treading water or pushing on to new records? If like-for-like sales figures are decreasing or standing still, you should seek an explanation. After all, growth companies are supposed to grow. What sort of press has the company been getting recently? Have there been enthusiastic reports about it in *Investors Chronicle*, the *Sunday Times* or on *The Money Programme*? Is the company's name on everybody's lips, or has nobody ever heard of them?

Has the chief executive announced a series of new contracts and purchases, or said nothing in the hope that nobody will notice that the growth has run out?

The company may be wonderful, but how is the sector doing?

You can use this information in a number of ways, of course. You might decide that the sector is upwardly mobile and so the company is 'onto a good thing' or you might decide that this may increase competition. You might also give extra credit to a company that have done exceptionally well in a poorly-performing sector or conclude that the lack of good news in the sector will 'get 'em in the end'.

As well as bothering about how particular sectors are behaving, how are the markets doing in general? Whether the bulls or the bears are ruling the FTSE-100 can have a big effect on the fate of a growth share. The almost unbroken bull run of the last few years has meant that 'up-to-date' testing of methods for identifying growth shares have not really been tested in a bear market. An opportunity for some research?

Questions, questions and more questions. Have you got the stamina to evolve a system of your own? Nobody ever said that picking a great growth share would be easy, but the financial avalanche that can start to come your way if you *do* manage to crack it can make a few hours' hard graft well worth it. Get to it.

Selling A Growth Share

We've seen above how you can have some hope of spotting a growth share, but how do you pick the right time to sell? Growth shares are a bit like boy bands. One moment their stock is generating ever more frenzied interest and rising ever more rapidly, the next it falls out of favour and everybody bales out to land on the next passing fancy. So how *can* you try to judge when to take your profits and sell? As questions go, this is indeed a hard one. I hope that I have already convinced you that by far the most difficult aspect of online trading is knowing when to sell, and for a growth share it's even harder to determine the optimum time to cash in your chips and run laughing to the e-bank. Nevertheless, let's spend some time examining how we might go about closing the deal to our satisfaction.

PEG check

One of the best ways to judge when to sell a growth share that has done well is to keep a careful eye on the PEG. As we've noted above, the PEG is a many-edged weapon in that it reflects quite a number of different company qualities in a single measure. Just as a low PEG suggests a measure of insurance against temporary bad news and gives a promise of future growth, an increasing PEG tells you that some of this growth is being 'used up' and the share may be becoming more vulnerable to adverse news.

If you want to go down the automatic route, then you could decide to sell as soon as the PEG has (let us say) doubled from the nice low value that it enjoyed when you bought it. Like everything else concerned with PEGs this is not a universal panacea as it produces a one-dimensional 'sell' signal which may well be seriously flawed in its timing. Perhaps a better way of proceeding is to keep track of the PEG of a growth company and review the fundamentals every time it passes through some set barrier.

Trailing stop-loss

Of course, our old friend the trailing stop-loss is a crucial companion when it comes to selling growth shares. When you initially buy the share you may well want to impose a stop-loss. After all, smallcap and fledgling shares are by nature more risky than their bigger and more stable brothers and sisters. (To some extent, this is an advantage as it is this very volatility that you want to exploit for yourself.) So suppose that you're in the happy situation where the initial stop-loss has never been triggered and your growth share really has grown. Then setting a new moving stop-loss at say 10 per cent below the share's maximum price should mean that whatever happens you'll do well out of the share. Remember when you do this though that you'll have to keep quite a careful check on prices, as an unexpected profit warning or piece of adverse news can make the price of a growth shares dive *fast*.

Don't look at the share price graph!

Well of course when you've bought what you hope is a growth share you *should* look at the share price graph (and as many other key financial indicators as possible) as regularly as you can. All that I'm trying to point out is that unless you're very used to looking at share price graphs in the right sort of way, they can be a bit misleading.

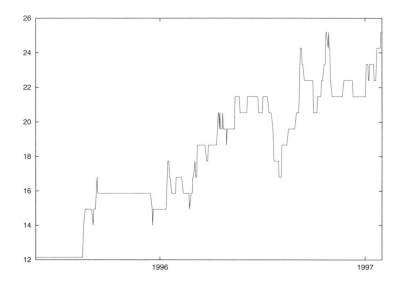

FIG. 6.2. MICE group share price, 1995–1997

The problem occurs when a growth share starts growing. Look at the share price graph in Figure 6.2 for exhibition equipment makers MICE group (a classic growth share) during 1995–1997. Should it put you off buying or make you sell?

If you're not careful, a little demon inside you will tell you that *the wiggly line has reached the top of the picture* and so *if that's the top then the share must be about to go down*. Don't listen! The whole point of a growth share is that it should keep on growing. The fact that the share price graph ends at the current high means nothing and you should base your decisions on other information. By the way, you might want to know how MICE group have done more recently. If you were duped into selling by Figure 6.2 then presumably you will be by Figure 6.3 as well!

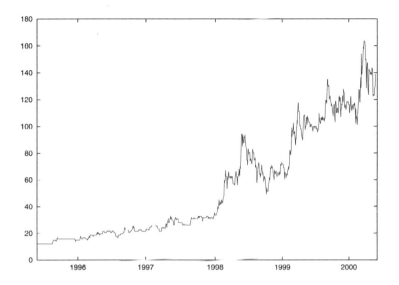

FIG. 6.3. MICE group share price, 1995–2000

Selling: the perennial problem

As we've said many times already, knowing when to sell is hard. With growth shares you're probably going to find it almost impossible to get out at the top with any regularity at all. The thing to do is to know this and understand it. Nobody ever went broke taking a profit, and although by now you're sure to understand the importance of running with your successes and cutting your losses, you have to accept that when you deal in growth shares you may often find that after you've sold (even for the best and most logical reasons) the price keeps shooting up. If you're going to give yourself a hard time and keep counting up all the money that you've 'lost' every time this happens then maybe you haven't got the stomach to monkey around with growth shares anyway. Above all, you must be pragmatic; if you trade growth shares you have to learn more than ever to take the rough with the smooth.

CASE STUDY

More Beer For The Boys

Let's end our brief discussion of growth shares by trying to put all the theory together in the form of a case study. Let me stress again that (like all the other case studies in this book) this was a *real* purchase. As you'll see, not many yachts were bought with the proceeds of this little flutter.

It's right at the end of October 1999 and it's situation normal: we're nosing around for growth shares. The 'safe-but-boring' part of our online portfolio is all buttoned up and we've just sold a small company at a nice profit when they triggered a 'sell' limit. Can we find a growth company that deserves our patronage share-wise?

A quick grub around all the web pages that allow one to work out PEGs has given us the interesting information that Springwood PLC (remember them from Table 6.1?) currently enjoy the encouragingly low PEG of 0.31. As we have seen above, a low PEG is not a guarantee of future sparkling performance, so let's investigate the company to see whether or not we should buy. Figure 6.4 shows the share price for the last few years and Table 6.2 contains most of the detailed financial data that we need to know (again, prospective figures are in bold type).

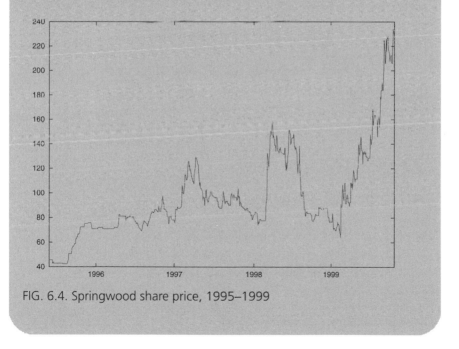

FIG. 6.4. Springwood share price, 1995–1999

First, some general information. Springwood (EPIC code SWO) are in the leisure sector and their business is operating nightclubs and pubs. All of their turnover comes from these operations and they are a 100 per cent UK operation. Their market cap is £51.5 million and this puts them in the 'fledgling' section of the indices. As usual, we've been on their tail for a while and have compiled our standard list of upside, neutral and downside reasons.

Upside reasons

■ That PEG. It's an attractive 0.31 and the prospective PER that's led to that value is only 15.2. The reason for the low PEG is the massive predicted growth: prospective GR is almost 50 per cent.

■ The company appears to be in good health as far as cash and borrowing are concerned. The net gearing is only 29 per cent which seems highly satisfactory for a company that's growing so fast. For the last four years, the cash flow per share has comfortably exceeded the capital expenditure per share and the last annual report also showed that cash flow per share exceeded EPS for the last trading year. All of these facts point to a company that manages its cash well and knows how to turn sales into real money.

■ Without a doubt, the share has upward momentum. Its relative strengths have been +155 per cent over the last year, +127 per cent over the last six months, +49 per cent over the last three months and +9 per cent over the last month. Relative strength is known to be a very important measure of the effectiveness of a growth share, and the fact that these figures have been turned in against a background of general torpor in the leisure and hotels sector make it clear that the company really does have something special.

■ How are pubs and clubs going to do in the near future? Are you joking? The millennium will be upon us soon, and there's going to be a nation-wide party. And where do people party? In pubs and clubs!

Year	1994	1995	1996	1997	1998	**1999**	**2000**
Turnover (£m)	16.1	14.2	17.0	14.5	9.78		
Pre-tax profit (£m)	−0.45	0.35	0.93	1.48	1.57	**2.51**	**4.00**
ROCE (%)	−2.40	8.46	7.25	9.47	9.86		
EPS (p)	−5.38	4.21	6.05	6.47	7.10	**11.5**	**16.9**
Dividend per share (p)	0	0	0.6	1.0	1.5	**2.4**	**4.0**
Dividend cover	–	–	10.1	6.5	4.7	**4.8**	**4.2**
Capex per share (p)	1.4	1.4	3.4	4.4	6.5		
Cash flow per share (p)	−4.14	25.6	5.9	10.5	12.0		

Latest and prospective figures:	
PER	**15.2**
PEG	**0.31**
ROCE	9.86%
Profit margin	18.1%
Gearing	29%
Dividend yield	**1.53%**
PTBV	3.59
PSR	5.26
Quick ratio	0.29
Current ratio	0.34

TABLE 6.2. Key financial data for Springwood (November 1999)

- Does the company have some sort of edge? Well one thing that stands out straight away is the huge margins that Springwood command. Their current profit margin is just over 18 per cent and not many other companies in the leisure sector (or any other sector, come to that) do as well as this. A little further work is necessary to establish whether this figure is a one-off or the result of a trend. A spot of judicious surfing is enough to confirm that margins were 4 per cent in 1995, 7 per cent the next year, and 12 per cent and 18 per cent in 1997 and 1998 respectively. High margins have therefore been slowly building up as sales increase and seem sustainable. Excellent.

- Most of the broker's consensus figures have been accurate recently, and when they've been a little out, the brokers have had to adjust by revising their estimates up rather than down; a good sign. Needless to say, the brokers' final estimates are a unanimous 'BUY'.

- Looking at the last annual report we find that the company chairman does not seem to be an individual given to wild exaggeration. Then again, why should he be? His company has a great set of figures and simply stating them and letting them speak for themselves is probably his best strategy. For this reason his talk of 'substantial increases in sales' coupled with 'sales remaining strong and in line with expectations' is strangely comforting.

As far as going forward is concerned, it's clear that stagnation is not an option. We learn that the company is about to open its largest ever venture, a club in Derby with a capacity of almost 3000, and has also opened a new office 'to accommodate the expanding operations and development of the company'. Music to our ears.

Neutral reasons

- The company profile has not been high recently and there appears to have been little news (good or bad) on its activities in the media.
- There seems to have been no buying or selling by the directors recently.
- It's a little hard to anticipate what will happen on New Year's Eve. Will sales be massive or will everybody be watching the fireworks? As none of us have ever seen in a new millennium before, we'll have to pass on this one. Of course the millennium bug may cause a global nuclear holocaust and none of this will matter. Since you're here reading this though, I guess that things weren't too bad.

Downside reasons

- When you're trying to assess any growth company's data it generally pays to be ultra-distrustful, and therefore to regard anything that's not immediately explainable as a downside. Let's just focus again on a particular part of the company data, which is shown for convenience in Table 6.3.

Year	1994	1995	1996	1997	1998	*1999*	*2000*
Turnover (£m)	16.1	14.2	17.0	14.5	9.78		
Pretax profit (£m)	−0.45	0.35	0.93	1.48	1.57	**2.51**	**4.00**
EPS (p)	−5.38	4.21	6.05	6.47	7.10	**11.5**	**16.9**
Growth rate (%)	-	-	43.7	6.94	9.74	**62.2**	**46.8**

TABLE 6.3. Springwood: why the drop in turnover?

What's going on here? Turnover appears to have dropped but EPS and profits have increased. Nine times out of ten increasing EPS and profits are caused by the simple expedient of *selling more stuff*. This does not seem to have happened here though. As noted already, what *has* happened is that margins have increased, and this is where the increase in EPS has come from. Is this a major downside? We conclude that it needn't be, but resolve to keep our eyes firmly trained on the company's profit margin.

■ The PEG is very small, but part of the reason for this is the fact that the growth rate is large. In fact it's close to 50 per cent and it's hard to believe that this can be sustained for very long. Should alarm bells be ringing? Let's try to find out by doing a few quick 'what-if' calculations. First, suppose that sometime soon the share price rises by 20 per cent, EPS stays the same, but the prospective growth rate shrinks to say 35 per cent. The new PER would be 1.2 × 15.2 = 18.2 and this would give a new PEG of 18.2/35 = 0.52, which is still an encouragingly low figure. Finally, suppose that earnings per share are 20 per cent less than expected, the price rises by 30 per cent and prospective growth slows to a measly 30 per cent. A quick sum then reveals that the new

PEG would be 0.82; disappointing, but not a major problem. We conclude that although the large growth rate has to be monitored, it does not seem to be a reason in itself not to buy the share.

■ We've already sung the praises of the very high margins that Springwood can command, and even satisfied ourselves that this is not a statistical anomaly of some sort but rather the end product of a real and sustainable trend. What is a little mystifying, however, is the fact that ROCE is under 10 per cent, which is pretty low for the sector. Good margins and a high ROCE usually go together for growth shares, so what's happening here? Closer examination yields no answers: there seem to be no reasons why ROCE is so comparatively low. On the basis that things that can't be explained are downright *bad*, this must be rated as a worrying downside.

■ This is a fledgling share, not a blue chip. Sure, it's got some great numbers, but it's risky.

■ Springwood is in the restaurant, pubs and breweries sector, which has not exactly been a star performer recently. The sector weighted average relative strength is 8 per cent down over the previous month and 17 per cent down over the previous year.

The final recommendation

The upsides outweigh the downsides by so much that we have to buy. Springwood seems to have a vibrant product which attracts very large profit margins. The fundamentals are nearly all good for a growth share and apart from a slight worry over turnover and the sector performance in general everything seems to be right. Since the market cap of the firm is small, we'll be careful and set a stop-loss at 200p.

Result

Bought 2000 SWO at 244p on 1 November 1999. By December 1999 the price was hovering around 275p. Decision taken to hold. Just before the end of the year, it dropped back down to 235p, only to rise again to 275p in February 2000. Again decided to hold. On 24 January 2000 the company confirmed that it had recently bought 1.3 million shares in Kingfisher Leisure and expressed an interest in making an offer for the rest. This was an exciting move as the acquisition of Kingfisher Leisure would have made Springwood a major force in the pub and club game. Decision taken to hold the shares *again*. By 25 January 2000 as much as 9.3 per cent of Kingfisher's shares had been bought and positive noises were still being made about buying them out.

After that it was downhill all the way. On 10 March 2000, it was announced that an offer for Kingfisher Leisure would 'not be in the best interests of its shareholders'. Just to add insult to injury, the Government's announcement of the possible introduction of legislation allowing 24-hour opening of pubs had the effect of making all the companies that operate nightclubs complain that this would adversely affect their trade: how could they carry on charging £3 a pint at 1am if the pub down the road was open? The shares hit the stop-loss rapidly after that and were sold at a loss.

Should we have sold when the price hit 275p? Maybe, but we thought that the shares had more in them. This was a decision made for the right reasons which was overtaken by events. For growth shares, *c'est la vie*.

Health Warning

Finally, let's sound a word of caution. If you haven't had quite a bit of experience trading online in FTSE-100 and Mid-250 companies then you should seriously question whether or not growth shares are for you yet. Being by nature companies at the smaller end of the market, there are inherent risks and you may lose a *lot* of money if things go awry. It's harder to keep track of small companies and there is not likely to be nearly so much information 'in the public domain' about them. The bigger a growth stock gets, the harder it is for it to keep up with itself and carry on expanding at the same rate. Very few shares keep on growing for ever, and it's often the case that when the price becomes much higher than it was only recently, it might only take a small piece of bad news to send the share back to whence it came. Growth share hunting is great fun: but be careful.

GROWTH SHARES

- Growth shares can yield large profits but are inherently more risky to buy than shares in larger and more stable companies.

- One of the keys to spotting a growth share is learning what a PEG is; another is understanding how to use it.

- The best methods for spotting growth shares don't use a company's PEG in isolation, but take into account many other business indicators as well.

- Judging when to sell a growth share is very hard indeed. Be realistic and don't chide yourself for not getting out at the top every time.

new issues,
AIM, OFEX and
foreign shares

Investing in new issues is a speculative business and
you should probably decide to specialise in it if you
want to have any chance of doing it effectively – AIM
and OFEX shares may be risky too.

Although this book is primarily about online share trading in plain straightforward British shares on the main London Stock Exchange, there are many other ways that you can acquire shares in an online fashion. These include buying new issues, buying shares on other British exchanges, and buying shares that trade in other countries. In this chapter we'll deal briefly with the mechanics of doing this and try to decide whether or not it's a good idea.

New Issues

Normally when you buy online you're buying shares from somebody else who wants to sell them. (If nobody *does* want to sell them, then bad luck: you can't buy. That's an illiquid market for you.) Sometimes, however, you get the chance to buy shares before anybody has ever bought them. Such opportunities come when companies 'float' and have a 'new issue' of shares. The point is that now this can be done online. When you've bought shares in a new company, these can then be added to your online portfolio via your stock transfer facility and traded with your e-broker just like any other shares that you may own. So how does one go about buying new issues online? Is it a good idea, and if so, what should one look out for?

Before discussing the details, pros and cons of investing online in new issues, let's have a quick history lesson. In the 1980s, everybody understood new issues. This is essentially what used to happen.

- Mrs Thatcher picked some sort of service or industry that Labour had nationalised in the 1960s or 1970s and announced that they were up for sale.

- A series of advertisements involving 'lovable characters that everybody could identify with' appeared in the newspapers and on television.
- The public scraped together what money they could and sent off for some shares. (Some sent away for the offer prospectus first but hardly anybody bothered to read it – after all, everybody knew what would happen.)
- There was a ballot and if you were lucky you were allowed to buy some shares (though in most cases far fewer than you originally applied for).
- The shares started trading at a far higher price than you had paid for them. Most people holding the shares shouted 'hurrah', sold them for a quick profit and decided that flotations were a good thing, and that they'd vote for Mrs Thatcher again provided that Britain won the odd war from time to time.
- (Sometimes) naughty people that had made multiple applications for shares using the names of relatives, dead people, racehorses, etc. got caught and fined or sent to prison. Sometimes these people were MPs.
- All the people that didn't sell and take an instant profit saw the value of their shares appreciate in a disgustingly healthy manner. Political commentators noticed this and complained that the 'sell-off had been too cheap'.
- Everybody waited for the process to begin again; the wait was not normally a long one.

Flotations, huh? Simple! Actually, it got even simpler in the 1990s when all the building societies started to float. This time, there was normally no ballot and you didn't even have to look out for the offer details; basically your building society just sent you shares for free.

As a result of all these free gifts being flung around, many people wrongly believed that flotations are always a good thing for the company involved and are also always a good thing for the lucky people that get the shares. However, not all flotations succeed, people that buy shares in flotations often get their fingers burned, and some businesses that survive the birth of flotation do not even make it to puberty as a company.

We therefore need to address the question: now that it's possible to buy flotation shares online (see below), and it's also clear that new issues are not the gravy train that they once were, is it worth your time, effort and money to invest in any of them?

Types of new issue

Before we can get down to the business of discussing what your e-trading strategy should be with regard to new issues, it's necessary to understand what different forms a flotation can take. There are actually quite a few ways in which a company can get itself a 'listing' (i.e. become a member of one of the recognised exchanges). These include the following.

■ **Flotation:** the procedure whereby an issuer makes shares available to the public, normally for the first time.

■ **Intermediaries offer:** a method of getting a share a listing which does not involve the issue of any new shares.

■ **Offer for sale:** the general public are offered, on behalf of a vendor, the opportunity to buy shares at a fixed price. The shares that are offered *already exist* (and the buyers therefore have to pay stamp duty).

■ **Offer for subscription:** the general public are offered, on behalf of a vendor, the opportunity to buy *new* shares at a fixed price. No stamp duty is thus payable.

- **Placing:** shares are offered to certain 'favoured' investors (usually people known to the broker). The shares may either be new or already exist. Needless to say, the 'old boy network' operates here and the general public usually never get a look in.
- **Subscription:** the same as an 'offer for sale'.

It is worth noting the differences between all of these contrasting ways that a company can be officially born on one of the exchanges. Essentially, up until a few years ago, nearly all new issues that were not privatisations of large utilities were effectively placings. There were publications where you could find out who was floating and what they were floating, but the process was largely a semi-secretive one and it was the devil's own job to get in on the act.

Now, of course, everything has changed. Like most other things that we take for granted now, the world wide web has led to many more opportunities for private and online investors to join the party. So how do you go about investigating new issues, what information is available, and what should you look out for?

New issues on the web

If you're interested in getting involved with new issues, then there's one website that you must know about. **www.issuesdirect.com** was set up solely to co-ordinate investment in new issues, and seems to work pretty well at doing just that. Issuesdirect handle a good number of the flotations that occur each quarter and have proved themselves in the past to be a reliable and efficient organisation.

The process is simple. First, go to their website and read about them carefully. If

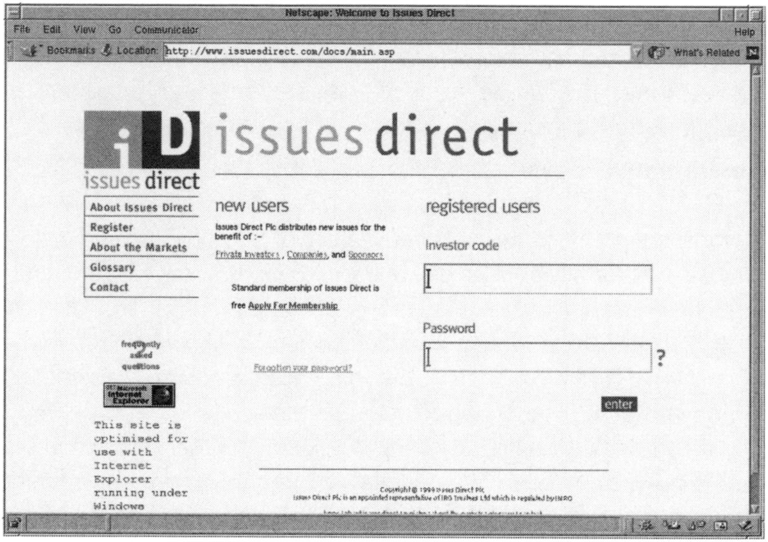

FIG. 7.1. The issuesdirect website

you decide to register then simply fill in the online form and submit it. Registration is free, and after a few days, confirmation that the process is complete should come through by e-mail. You'll be given some more details of how the site works, and a username and a password that will allow you to access details of forthcoming flotations.

If you decide that you're interested in buying into a flotation, then the normal procedure is to download the prospectus of the company from the issuesdirect website. At the same time, you should be able to download an application form, which will allow you to apply for shares. The prospectus and the application form download as .pdf files, which your computer may not be able to handle. To read them, you need a piece of software called Adobe Acrobat, but this is no problem as you can download it free by just following the onsite instructions.

If you finally decide to give a new issue a go, then you should fill in the application form and send it off with the requisite cheque. At present, this part of the process is not electronic and requires using the dreaded paper/post combination. You should also understand that many firms cash your cheque as soon as they receive it and pay you back later if the money is not used, so it's unwise to try to finesse your cash flow situation at the bank. Eventually though (subject to ballots if the issue is oversubscribed) you should get the share certificates in the post. If you don't have plans to sell the shares straight away to (hopefully) make a quick killing then send the share certificate off to your online broker as soon as possible so that you can have the stock registered in your e-trading account.

Issuesdirect is not the only website that deals with new share issues (though at the moment it seems to be the best). Brokers Durlacher run an interesting site at **www.nothing-ventured.com** which, as you might have guessed from the name, specialises in Internet startup and other tech-related companies. Although this site is definitely worth a look if you're interested in new issues, you should be clear that many of the new issues featured on the site are highly speculative and consequently highly risky. Of course, they can yield huge profits as well if you strike it lucky. You have been warned. Electronic public offerings are also co-ordinated by EPO at **www.epo.com** and if you're interested in new issues then this is undoubtedly a site worth visiting.

FIG. 7.2. The nothing-ventured website – only for the brave!

What to look for in new issues

As usual, investigating new issues online is the easy part: actually deciding whether to buy into them or not is the tough bit. One of the biggest problems is that it's so hard to give any general guidelines. During a typical year, companies of every description float on the full exchange, AIM and OFEX. Some will eventually make it and some will crash and burn in spectacular and expensive style. Investing in new issues is a speculative business and you should probably decide to specialise

FIG. 7.3. The EPO website

in it if you want to have any chance of doing it effectively. Here are some general guidelines, however.

■ Whatever you do *download and read the prospectus*. In fact don't just read it, dissect it. Normally you're not going to be able to get your hands on nearly as much data as you would before you decide to buy a share in an existing company, so you must make the most of every nugget of information contained in the prospectus. If there's a website, then of course you should check that out too.

■ Give preference to companies that are floating after a long and sustained history of growth and profitability; with new issues, a track record counts for a lot. For example, when the investment banking company Beeson Gregory gained a full listing in April 2000, they were not a 'start-up' company. Their business record was already exemplary, they had a fine brand name within the financial industry and could point to a strong past record of growth in turnover, profits and EPS. Investing in a new issue like Beeson Gregory is thus a completely different matter from putting your money into something like an Internet startup company.

- Be wary of companies that are floating on AIM rather than on the full exchange. Even if they do well you may find that the spreads are so large that it's almost impossible to make much of a profit when you come to sell.

- Be clear what your tactics are before you invest. Are you buying for the medium or long term, or are you out for a quick profit via a quick sell? If the latter is your game, then remember that the share certificates may not actually arrive until a few days after the flotation takes place, and this may make them awkward to sell.

- If you think that you might be likely to take part in the great new issues game, shadow some new issues before you start to play. Get some idea of how new shares behave in the first week after they are issued, what sort of volatility you can expect and what kinds of factors influence the price. Conduct some experiments of your own with pretend money before risking the real thing.

- Don't fall into the trap of thinking that just because previous flotations in a specific area were successful, then the next one is bound to be as well. Judge each company on its own merits using as many fundamentals and as much basic data as you can find.

- Be very careful when you read bulletin boards and chat pages that purport to give 'inside information' on flotations. Most people that *really* have inside information don't share it as they want as much of the new issue as possible for themselves. More nonsense and downright misinformation is spread on the web about new issues than about almost any other sort of share.

- Do your sums carefully when you decide how many shares to apply for. If you actually want to buy £2000-worth of a new issue and you hear that they are oversubscribed then you may be tempted to send off an application form for say £4000 in the hope that you'll get what you wanted in the first place. Remember though that you might actually end up spending £4000 on shares if things don't go exactly to plan.

- Before you buy, try to make a realistic assessment of the risks involved and assess what failure will mean for your portfolio. There's nothing wrong with risking a few bob on a highly speculative start-up company, but don't risk breaking the back of your online portfolio for a new issue.

Talking of flotations, what sort of exchanges do new companies float on, and how do these exchanges operate?

AIM and OFEX

Lots of the companies that we know, love and buy and sell on a regular basis today started their lives as AIM or OFEX companies. Most e-brokers will also allow you to trade AIM and/or OFEX companies online (though some require you to ring them up and will not carry out the whole process electronically). So is it worth trading shares on these markets?

Ultimately you have to make your own decision about where your money goes, and if you decide to run a portfolio that combines blue chips and other more risky shares then AIM or OFEX may be just to place to find your 'outsiders'. Before investing any cash though, you ought to know something about how these smaller exchanges operate.

AIM

Let's look first at AIM (the Alternative Investment Market). AIM was set up in 1995 and was designed specifically to meet the needs of smaller, fast-growing companies who wanted to float but did not meet the criteria for a full listing on the stock exchange. AIM was created by, and has always been regulated by the London Stock Exchange. AIM companies are not bound by UK listing authorities listing rules and are thus swimming in a more flexible regulatory environment. This has its advantages and disadvantages; the main plus point for a company is that their profile increases and everybody can trade their shares. If the company does well, then in time it can aspire to a full listing. The chief disadvantage of course is that the criteria that the main stock exchange insists upon for listing are there for a very good reason. Some AIM companies which can never hope to reach the sort of stability that is required for a full listing therefore tend to go bust rather speedily.

Figure 7.4 shows how AIM as an index has performed since its launch. You'll note that essentially AIM showed little growth during its first few years but benefited greatly from the dot.com boom. Needless to say, things returned to normal after the techno-slaughter of spring 2000.

Currently, AIM comprises about 360 companies from a large variety of sectors. Since 1995 about 60 companies have progressed from puberty on AIM to a fully-grown-up full listing. There are certainly good companies trading on AIM, but there are also many bad ones. The challenge is to pick the plums and dispense with the lemons.

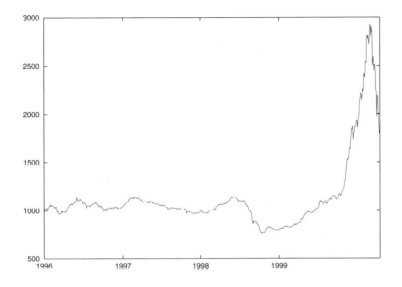

FIG. 7.4. The AIM index since 1996

OFEX

OFEX started on 2 October 1995 and was originally a medium to allow share dealing in the 45 companies whose shares had previously been traded under the now defunct rule 4.2 of the London Stock Exchange. OFEX has grown into a market for shares that are not quoted on the London Stock Exchange. Unlike AIM, OFEX is not run by the London Stock Exchange, but by J. P. Jenkins Ltd, who act as the market maker. They have ultimate power and can suspend trading in any OFEX share at any time for any reason, although if this happens it is usually to ensure an orderly market.

The major problem in trading some OFEX and some AIM shares is the sometimes disastrous illiquidity of the market, although most securities traded do so on a firm price. These are not large liquid companies. All OFEX companies are obliged to appoint a CREST-complaint registrar. Trades are therefore matched using CREST, although some have to be settled via a residual stock transfer form method.

The liquidity of small companies can be poor as few institutional investors become active in tiddlers. In both OFEX, AIM and even some illiquid listed securities it can be difficult to deal and liquidity may disappear. These shares can also be volatile and the price may be affected by small transactions.

At the current time nobody is able to offer true online dealing in OFEX, although it is believed that OFEX will provide electronic links to brokers, allowing online trading shortly. OFEX currently has 218 companies traded on it, and has supplied over 36 companies to AIM and 8 straight to the Official List. OFEX is also home to some well-known companies such as Weetabix and Arsenal.

The sorts of things that AIM shares do

To show you the sort of game that you might be getting into if you decide to trade AIM shares, let's take a quick look at a couple of AIM companies. All figures are from August 1999 and, as usual, all were found on the web in only a few minutes.

Albemarle & Bond had the very good idea of reviving traditional pawn broking, making it a bit more upmarket, and providing a cheque cashing service at the same time. They have become so successful that there might well be an Albemarle & Bond second-hand jewellery shop in your high street. The market cap of the company is £19 million, and the 1998 annual report showed a pretax profit of £1.93 million from a turnover of £7.20 million. Their dividend has increased

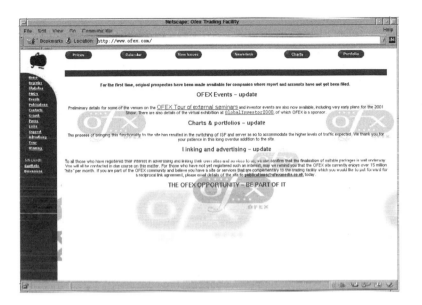

FIG. 7.5. The OFEX website

year on year, as has EPS. The company's gearing hovers at around 48 per cent, a very reasonable figure for a company of this size. The interest cover is a healthy 8.1, the dividend cover is 3.7 and the quick ratio is 1.62. On a prospective PER of 10.7 and great ROCE and profit margin figures of 25 per cent and 31 per cent respectively, the company seems to be a well-run, successful outfit. The 1998 annual report showed a cash flow per share of 0.85p as opposed to a capex per share of 1.32p. It would be nice to see a bit more cash flow, but year-on-year growth seems to be encouragingly good. The share price is shown in Figure 7.6.

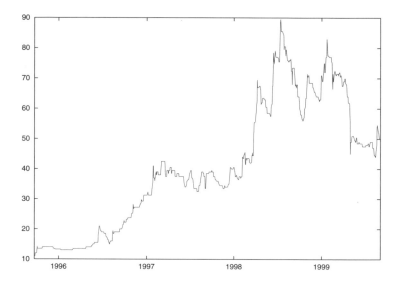

FIG. 7.6. Albemarle & Bond share price

You don't need to be a rocket scientist to notice exactly how volatile the share price has been. In particular, in spite of superficially good results the August 1999 price of 47p is well down on the 1999 high of 83p. We conclude that *even for a seemingly well-run and stable company*, the volatility of an AIM share is likely to be high. Just one final note: if you thought that the shares were a buy at 47p, then be aware that you'd have paid 49p per share to buy, and shares could have been sold for 45p. I'll leave it to you to add the stamp duty and commission and work out how much the share price would have to move before you made any money.

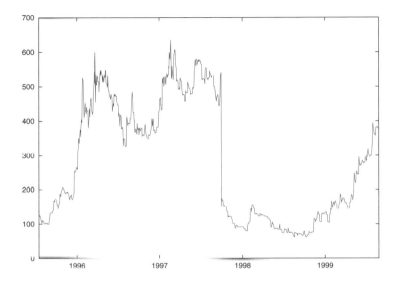

FIG. 7.7. SR Pharma share price

SR Pharma carry out research and development for pharmaceutical products. With a market cap of £65.8 million they are actually the 868th largest listed company in Britain. In 1999, their turnover was £0.21 million and the 1998 annual report shows a pretax loss of £1.58 million. The prospective PER is −41.9, ROCE and MARGIN are −47 and −906 respectively and the company's gearing is −109 per cent. The chairman has recently made a few recent bullish statements, and the normalised EPS is predicted to rise in 2000 to −6.50p. As for the share price, Figure 7.7 tells the full grisly story. The shares traded at around 600p (with a maximum price of 635p) for most of 1997, plummeted briefly to 62p in 1998, started 1999 at 104p and are now rising towards 400p.

Do you really want to get involved in games of this sort? Can you see any reason at all why SR Pharma shares have moved like this? Before the company's chief executive starts issuing law suits against me for libel, let me make my position clear. As far as I know, SR Pharma are a wonderful company who may one day carry out the R&D for a drug that eventually saves my hide and the lives of many others. In ten years' time they may be a pillar of the pharmaceutical establishment and be in many online portfolios as a blue chip. But from these figures, how are we to tell?

It's hard enough to try to predict what will happen to the share price of big, stable companies. Although under the right circumstances I might *just* contemplate having a flutter on Albemarle & Bond, investing in a company like SR Pharma is nearer to a complete guess than I ever want my money to be involved in. You pay your money and you take your choice. With AIM and OFEX shares though you can win or lose a great deal and you had better be absolutely clued up about the risks and downsides before you dip your toe in the water.

Trading Foreign Shares

The London Stock Exchange may be the second largest in the world (only the NYSE is bigger), but there are exchanges in just about every major (and some distinctly minor) financial centre on the globe. From the Nikkei in Japan through the Hang Seng in Hong Kong via the something-in-cyrillic in Uzbekistan to the Brazilian Bovespa, market makers the world over are beavering away and investors just like you and me are placing their bets and hoping for the best. So does the internationalism of shares and share dealing have any important consequences for online traders in the UK?

What's the greatest advantage of the Internet as a medium of communication? Evidently the answer is that no matter where you are physically situated you have access to every website in the world. It matters not whether the site was designed in Europe, Asia, Australasia or anywhere else: access is (nearly) instant and (nearly) free for everybody. Surely it should therefore follow that there ought to be *somebody* out there who will allow me to trade online in shares from the Brazilian stock exchange? In theory, yes: in practice, probably not at the moment. As you'll know if you've ever tried to do it, it's often actually quite hard to buy shares that trade on foreign markets even if you use a traditional bank or broker, and even if it's not hard it's usually expensive. The situation from an electronic trading point of view is that there are a *few* sites (for example www.e-cortel.com) that offer online facilities for buying in other countries, but in general you'll have to try quite hard to buy foreign shares online in real time.

This state of affairs cannot continue for long. It can be only a few months before British investors can buy European and US shares online. The next section explains why.

Foreign Shares: Death To The FTSE!

If you're looking for one single example of a typical behavioural feature that large and successful companies have exhibited over the last 20 years, it has to be the tendency to seek mergers, take over each other, buy up each other, and generally sweep up a lot of medium-sized companies together to make one whopping great multinational. For a while now there have been rumours and hints that the same sort of thing is likely to happen as far as stock exchanges are concerned, so perhaps it should have been no surprise that in May 2000 the London Stock Exchange announced that it was merging with the Frankfurt Bourse to form a new consolidated exchange called iX. Despite the fact that in September 2000 the London Stock Exchange pulled out of the planned merger the case illustrates the point.

Needless to say, the merger trend is not limited to Germany and the UK. France, Holland and Belgium have announced a link up, Norway, Sweden and Denmark have joined forces and the NASDAQ is reported to be 'establishing a bridgehead' in London.

The big question, of course, is what's it all going to mean in practical terms for online traders? At present, nobody knows. It will only be possible to really judge the effect that these sweeping changes will have after the new mergered exchange has been up and running for a year or so. No doubt good and bad points of the new system will emerge, but for now the best that we can do is to point out some of the open questions that are posed by the 'iX plan'. For example:

- Will British companies be forced to trade only in Euros?
- If British companies do decide to trade in Euros, how will online investors cope with the double jeopardy involved in trying to predict not only how their shares will perform, but also how the Euro will fare against the pound?
- The Euro? Isn't that the one with the downhill-all-the-way value chart? Will the Euro even still be around when iX is launched?
- Will online dealing commissions go down as a result of the new plans?
- Will spreads reduce as a result of the new exchange? (Werner Seifert, the chief executive of iX says that they will.)

- Since Britain is almost unique in charging its share buying public stamp duty will we at last be able to rid ourselves of this annoyance? (After all, stamp duty is not payable on foreign share purchases.)
- What will happen to UK tracker funds? Will they start to invest in the new European indices or stick to British companies?

Is iX merely the thin end of the wedge? Almost certainly. Early in June 2000, the birth of GEM (the Global Equity Market) was announced. Conceived partly as a response to growing popularity of Internet trading and partly because of the news of the formation of iX, GEM is to be created around the NYSE, the Tokyo Stock Exchange, the Euronext alliance of Paris, Amsterdam and Brussels and the exchanges of Mexico, Toronto, Australia, Brazil and Hong Kong. This will allow continuous 24-hour trading in big-name, international stocks.

Although it will be a while before the plans for GEM crystallise, some stupefying figures are already being bandied about. You are invited to gasp in amazement at a predicted total market capitalisation of $20 trillion and a total of 60 per cent of all global traded equity. Impressive though these numbers may be, what will be done about tricky issues like uniformisation of accounting standards, possible liquidity problems when trading outside one's home time zone and conflicting tax laws? Discussions about GEM are only just beginning and there is obviously a long way to go, but the fact that the NASDAQ opened for business in Osaka, Japan on 19 June 2000 is an unmistakable pointer to the impending globalisation of online share trading.

Very few people are smart enough to be able to guess exactly what will happen when iX comes on stream in Autumn 2000. Even fewer can have a clue how things might work out if GEM becomes a reality. One thing is for sure, however: it's tough enough picking the right shares from the UK market. How much harder is it going to be when hundreds of European, US and Asian firms are involved as well?

NEW ISSUES, AIM AND OFEX

- New issues are not the soft touch that they once were; tread carefully.

- If you're thinking of buying into a new issue you must use every bit of information that you can lay your hands on to decide whether or not it's worth investing.

- AIM and OFEX shares may be highly volatile. Although they can offer the prospect of rapid profits the associated large spreads and illiquidity can sometimes be major problems.

- A 24-hour a day global exchange seems inevitable.

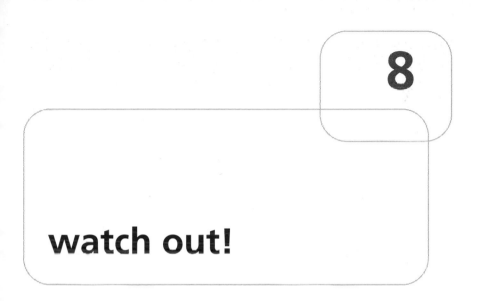

8

watch out!

Don't give up your day job!

There are a few things that you should watch out for. To be precise, there are some general things, and there are some more specific things. The general things have been grouped below in sections, and the specific things have been put in a section all of their own entitled 'the ten deadly sins of online share trading'. Some of these sins don't only apply to online trading: many also apply to ordinary trading. Here's a (fairly) interesting fact: after I wrote the 'ten deadly sins' I read that excellent book *The Motley Fool UK Investment Guide*. I was interested to see that they also listed 'the ten most common investing mistakes'. In some cases, the two lists coincided, but in others they were different. Read that book as well and see how the two lists compare.

Don't Believe All That You Surf

One of the beauties of the Internet is that it holds so much information. Almost overnight, we have gone from a prehistoric dark age where only the lucky few had access to what they needed to inform their financial dealings to a brave new world where 99 per cent of all the information that anybody could ever need is both easy to find and free. In one sense though, the very freedom that makes the Internet such a valuable resource is also its own Achilles heel. The problem is that (barring things that are so nasty that they are actually illegal) *anybody* can post *anything* on the Internet.

This freedom of speech leaves the unscrupulous with rather too many ways in which they can screw things up for the rest of us. Some of the simpler ruses are obvious. For example, suppose that I buy shares in miaowpoo.com, a preposterous 'Internet' company which sells cat toilets online. Presumably if

I then pepper every bulletin board and shares chat room with rumours about how this feline firm are about to be taken over by ARM holdings, merge with Baltimore or be bought up by Thus and are 'the latest hot investment', others may buy the shares as well. If enough others buy the shares, then guess what – they go up! Great: now I can sell and watch all the other poor suckers go down the er … litter tray.

Of course, I could also operate the other way around. If I spot a company that's genuinely a good buy but whose shares are too expensive for my taste at the moment, then a few good rumours of 'boardroom dissent' and 'an impending profit warning' should send them on the slide. When the price has fallen low enough, I buy and wait for my investment to appreciate.

Even worse, an unscrupulous company could employ touts to raid as many Internet chat rooms and bulletin boards as possible and pump up the shares. Or, if I worked in the City I could reveal 'insider trading' information to colleagues and friends via the Internet.

All of these are nasty, dishonest things to do but realistically, what can be done about them? In normal circumstances people voice their opinions all the time. Nevertheless, should they be prosecuted for these views if they post them on the Internet? By the same token, if I believe that a company is ripe for takeover and suggest another company that might do so, am I just a good judge or am I committing an offence?

It's almost impossible to make hard and fast rules about this sort of thing. The regulatory authorities have been considering this for a while, however, and it's likely that the special team set up by the FSA (Financial Services Authority) to scrutinise bulletin boards will be making their first arrests sometime soon. What effect this will have on the sort of misinformation that's out there at the moment is not so easy to quantify, but the very small number of successful insider trading prosecutions makes it likely that any legislation that finally makes its way to the statute books will be very hard to enforce.

In the meantime, be suspicious of everything that you read that has an element of opinion about it. Remember that there's usually safety in numbers and don't pay too much attention to people sounding off on the Internet on their own.

Don't Give Up Your Day Job

Look me in the eye and tell me that you're not going to take this online trading stuff too seriously. If you have a good job, keep it that way. For the vast majority of online share traders (like us) trading should be a hobby and an investment. Although I've said it before (and will say it again before the end of this book) *you don't have the skill* to take it too seriously. It therefore follows that if you try to make a living out of online trading then you are likely to be heading for financial oblivion.

The Ethics Of It All

One thing that you may need to watch carefully is the ethics of it all. In the end, you will have to decide for yourself if there are companies whose shares you will not buy purely for ethical reasons. The golden rule is simple: don't buy shares in a company that you feel unhappy about. Unfortunately the problem is normally that this is far easier said than done.

For example, we all know that smoking is bad for you and there is overwhelming statistical evidence that it will shorten your life. Nevertheless, smoking is not a crime and people have the right to decide whether to indulge in this particular habit or not. Would this make you refuse to buy BAT (British-American Tobacco) shares even if they were a dead cert for rapid growth? A public meeting of ethical investors would almost certainly agree that peddling a product that kills thousands of people every month is downright immoral, and decide that the shares were not for them. Well done, we say; congratulations on your stand. Off you go home to decide on something less harmful to put your money into. By the way, as you leave, are you driving? Being ethical, you'll be insured of course. What's that? You're insured with Eagle Star? Who are intimately connected with BAT? Something to ponder, perhaps!

The conflicts in ethical investing can seem to be never-ending. There are few companies that don't do things that don't upset *somebody*. What do you do if you find out that one of the directors of Totallynice plc is also a director of a company that sells land mines to Africa? How do you reconcile the fact that pharmaceutical companies save people's lives by developing new drugs, but kill animals (and sometimes humans) in the process? It's down to you to decide this and only you can be sure that your investment ethics will allow you to sleep soundly at night. It's worth thinking about though: after all, it's not unknown for companies who do really nasty things to go under because there are ethical people around. Sometimes, you really *can* make a difference.

Ethics Gone Mad

Here's another, more sinister, aspect of ethics that you may not have considered. How easy it is to keep your identity as a shareholder in a company secret? The answer, for a variety of reasons, is that it's almost impossible. The names of all shareholders (with the exception of those for whom shares are held in a nominee account or who own the share as part of a unit trust) in a company appear automatically on the share register. Worse, the addresses (and often the telephone numbers as well) of every shareholder appear on this register and anybody can look at it. Worse still, anybody can buy a copy to take away with them. In the US, it is common practice for companies to sell their share registers to the highest bidder as a profitable sideline. Needless to say, once the sale has taken place, targeted junk mail, junk phone calls and junk salesmen all follow with inevitable swiftness.

Junk mail is one thing, but lately there have also been occasions when people appearing on a shareholders' register have been the victims of deliberate scams. This is bad enough, but spare a thought for the shareholders of Huntingdon Life Sciences who all received orders from animal rights campaigners to sell their shares or risk having militant members of the organisation calling at their houses. What are they to do? They may have bought the shares for the best of reasons, but now they are being given ultimata by members of groups that have a reputation for bending the law at best and being downright violent at worst. If this can happen to Huntingdon Life Sciences, how long is it before SmithKline Beecham shareholders are intimidated in the same way? One can only conclude that some sort of legislation to give shareholders at least a measure of anonymity is well overdue.

The Ten Deadly Sins of Online Trading

This section is the Rue Morgue of Internet traders, the chamber of horrors of share dealers and the skeleton in the cupboard of serious investors. I can pretty well guarantee that if you avoid all of these deadly sins then you'll show a healthy profit. Unfortunately, I can also guarantee that all of us have been guilty of all of these horrors at some time. But steer clear of these mortal sins and your e-trading will feel the benefit.

SIN 1: not cutting losses

Cut your losses. Do it. I know that I've said this far too many times already in this book, but you have to get rid of your dogs if you want to survive the mean streets of the exchanges. 'It's bound to go up again eventually if I wait long enough' is the plaintive cry of the investor who's (nearly always) going to be disappointed come judgement day on the great dealing floor in the sky. Anyone who's dabbled in the world of share buying knows how tempting it is to sit on falling shares, pretending that they're not there and hoping that tomorrow will bring some respite. Partly it's a mental problem. Nobody likes to admit that they made a bad call, and by refusing to accept the obvious you tell yourself subconsciously that you were just unlucky, a victim of cruel fate, and that things will soon turn around for you. Nonsense. Just remember that *nobody ever said that the markets were fair*. It's bad luck but you can handle it if you deal with it properly. Quite apart from anything else, your remaining investment is *dead money*. It's going nowhere except down, and the sensible thing to do is free it from its unprofitable prison and send it on holiday with a share that deserves it.

Making a loss on Internet share dealing is a bit like getting a tennis ball between the legs: you can't quite understand what all the fuss is about until it happens to you. It hurts. Taking a loss makes you think in a whole different way about why you're trading. But you *must do it* if you are to have any chance of succeeding. Sometimes you decide to sell, get shot of your dog, take your loss in your stride, and then have to sit and watch aghast as the price leaps up. Forget it. You stuck to your guns and sold when you had to. These things happen, and no matter how much money you lost you did the right thing. Start cutting your losses – now.

SIN 2: thinking that you understand

They say that soccer teams are at their most vulnerable just after they've scored a goal, and a similar thing can apply to online traders. OK, so you've just clicked the mouse button and cashed out for a healthy profit. You're sitting back and enjoying the warm glow of satisfaction that only the delights of free money can bring, and that awful, pernicious thought starts to creep into your brain: 'I've got this stuff worked out: finally I understand how the markets work!'

If this particular demon ever comes tapping on your shoulder, then slap yourself on the face fast, because you're heading for trouble. How much do you really know or understand? I'll tell you: *Nothing*. Although you did your research carefully, came to an informed decision and backed your judgement you *may have simply been lucky*. You can never know a tenth as much as the traders, market makers and company directors, and even they haven't a clue what's happening most of the time. Heed the wise words of a famous successful investor who was asked by the bellboy of the top New York hotel where he was staying. 'Do you know what the markets will do today, sir?' His reply was deadpan: 'yep'. The bellboy was fascinated: 'So what *will* they do, sir?' 'They'll fluctuate'.

By the same token, don't buy things that you don't understand. It's been said many times previously in this book that you should try to become an expert in one particular area or sector and there's no doubt that expertise of this sort will always pay in the end. Even if you can't become a true expert though, don't dabble in shares that you know nothing of. Why buy Trafficmaster shares if you have no idea of what they make, why they have a competitive edge, what the in-car guidance system market has done recently or who their competitors are? As the good folk in Yorkshire say, if you know nowt then buy nowt.

Keep repeating to yourself 'I know nothing' and the sin of crediting yourself with omnipotence that has brought down so many will not be marked down in your own personal black book.

SIN 3: trading by the clock

Just because you've sold some shares and have some collateral in your e-trading account, it doesn't mean that you have to use it straight away to buy some more. You should buy when you judge that the time is right, and *not otherwise*.

Not many people make any money betting on horse races (and most of those that tell you that they do don't really: they just have selective memories) but you can tell the sure-fire losers by the fact that they turn up at the same time and the same place regularly. 'Having your Saturday flutter' may be an enjoyable bit of fun, but in the long run if you bet because it's time to bet rather than because it's *right* to bet, you'll lose money. It's just the same with shares, but with one important difference: if you just let your money lie fallow in your account, you actually gain on the deal anyway because of the interest that you make on it. You can't lose! (Except of course by spending it unwisely because of buying from habit rather than using sound reasoning to pick the right time to pounce.)

Talking of the clock, it's also a good idea to make it a rule that you do not trade just as the markets are kicking off for the day or just as they're about to go up to bed for the night. Large and unpredictable price changes can happen early in the morning or late at night, and you want to be insulated from these as far as possible. It's an interesting exercise to log on to whatever service you use to track your portfolio early in the morning or after trading has closed. You will often see price movements as early as 7.30am and as late as 5.30pm. It's also a good idea to be a bit wary of the third Friday of each month, since this is when most options expire (see chapter 9). This mass option expiry can lead to rapid and large changes in share prices as the option writers and hedge funds all seek to close their positions.

SIN 4: not being serious about security

Your e-trade account has *your* money in it; possibly lots of it! So it would be insane to be anything other than paranoid about security. First of all, you'll be offered the chance to use a number of different passwords for trading (for example, one to get into the site, one to access the trading page, and one to actually buy or sell shares). Don't be dumb and choose all these passwords to be the same to 'save trouble'! The security features are there to protect you: use them.

Remember, usually your passwords are the only protection that you have, so choose them carefully. Don't use names, dates, or even coherent words that could be looked up in a dictionary and make sure that all of your passwords are at least eight characters long. The ideal password consists of some numbers, some letters, and some symbols: something like 'f1g2-+sd' or '1(2.as56' is the sort of thing that you want to use. (Don't bother: neither of these is my real password!)

Don't tell your password to *anybody*. This might sound so obvious that it's hardly worth saying, but one of the major causes of computer hacking is nothing technological or clever: the victim just blabbed their password! When I say anybody, I *mean* anybody.

SIN 5: not realising the risks

When I talk about shares people often don't appreciate that there are real risks involved. Oh, they *think* that they do; in fact they all think that they're strong enough to swallow a big loss without complaining, but they don't really think that it'll ever happen to them. The trouble is, it can.

Part of the difficulty lies in the fact that for many people, their only share experience has been in windfalls and privatisations that virtually guarantee a quick profit. They've no real experience of profit warnings, downsizing and all the things that generally happen when companies go down the toilet. Now it's true that if you buy a dollop of say Abbey National shares, then, Abbey National being a blue chip, you're not going to lose all of your money. Unfortunately it's also true that Abbey National shares lost nearly 40 per cent of their value over the 'millennium end/millennium start' months. It's probable that eventually they'll regain all of their previous value, and then all that you will have lost will be the interest that would have accrued if you'd put the money into a bank (like Abbey National, say!) instead of buying the shares. So for blue chips it's normally just a matter of time.

For smaller (and hence much riskier) companies, things can be much worse. Here you really can lose virtually all of your money, and if it's money that was earmarked to pay some future mortgage or to send the kids to college, this is likely to have a severe effect on your life and lifestyle. In the end perhaps it really is true that you have to lose a large sum of your own to understand what it's like.

SIN 6: buying on a whim

Elsewhere in this book, I extol the virtues of having more than one reason for buying a particular share. Having just one reason is risky enough (though sometimes it's the right decision), but if your only justification for buying is that you heard some gossip down at the pub, or read a recommendation in the newspaper, or (even worse) got your 'hot tip' from a random Internet site, then you're heading for certain trouble.

As we noted earlier in the book, if you invest randomly in shares then on average you'll make money, so in one sense buying on a whim (and therefore virtually at random) is not such a great sin. The trouble is, it messes up your plans and leaves you in the sort of state of mind where you'll risk thousands of pounds at the drop of a hat. This just *can't* be good for your general strategy.

Furthermore, buying on a whim leaves you prey to the unscrupulous. Plenty of the 'experts' sounding off on the Internet own shares themselves, and many of them figure that if they can get you to buy the same share, then the share will rise. They may know absolutely nothing about the company or its business. Don't buy on a whim. Do your homework properly and make it happen for you for the *right* reasons.

SIN 7: chasing profits by numbers

Say you've had a few successful weeks, and made a tidy profit. Wouldn't it be nice to repeat the dose? After all, if you could make that sort of money again in that sort of time, it'd only be three more weeks until you had enough to buy that shiny new car. Let's see; what sort of share might do that for us. . . ? *Don't plan this way*. You have to realise that profits come when they jolly well want to come, and usually some losses have to be taken on the way. Unless you've got second sight, you have no control over how quickly things will move and how much the price will change. If you set yourself targets like 'make £x every week', then since there's no sensible strategy that can achieve this, it follows that you must be buying and selling for mainly the wrong reasons. This is just making this harder for yourself and in the long run can only lead to trouble.

Of course, *long-term planning* is fine. For example, if you put £5000 in your e-trading account initially and made £500 profit in your first year of trading, then it is entirely reasonable to try to double this by putting another £5000 into your account. Just remember: even the top managed funds think long term and never try to predict their profits from week to week.

SIN 8: guessing every click

The stick market 'clicks' thousands of times every day, and even blue chip shares move with many of the clicks. Dealing charges are so low at many e-trade sites (though of course there's still the stamp duty and the spread) that you might be tempted to buy large quantities of shares, hope that they will rise quickly by a small amount, and then sell for a small but positive profit. This strategy is close to day trading, and in my opinion it's a poor strategy. *Nobody* can predict what will happen at each click, and buying and selling so rapidly puts your effective dealing costs up hugely. Also, though you might be prepared to sell for only a 1 or 2 per cent gain, would you be equally prepared to sell to realise a small loss? I doubt it.

There will probably be times when you buy and sell a share in a single week, and there may even be times when you buy and sell in a single day. But the general view that the markets are for the long term and not the short term is a sound one and you should try to respect it wherever possible.

SIN 9: Obsession

Why did you decide to start online trading? I hope that it was mostly for fun, with the added carrot of some money to be made. If it's not fun, then you'd better either be very good at it or stop doing it. If you're constantly losing money, then stop doing it (or better, read this book again). Whatever happens, don't let your online trading become an obsession. If you ever find yourself in a position where it's all that you ever think about, or you start to awake from sleep wondering if two companies will merge, or your temper and mood depend only on how your trading's going, then take a long, hard look at yourself and digest what you see. Is the whole business getting too much of a hold of you? Of course there's no harm in being interested, enthusiastic, or even fascinated by online trading, but if this turns to obsession then not only will your quality of life rapidly diminish, but your trading acumen and reasoning will probably become seriously flawed as well.

SIN 10: not keeping records

Keep records of *everything*. There are two main reasons why not keeping proper records will lead you astray, one operational and one strategic. Operationally speaking, if you trade shares online you are going to have to give some consideration to your tax position. This should not really be a problem, but it's essential that you keep as many records as you can for the Inland Revenue. For this reason alone, every time I buy or sell anything I print out the contract note and the corresponding snapshot of my account details just before and just after the transaction has been completed. I also regularly review my online account to see what charges have been made and what interest and dividends have accrued.

There is also a strategic reason why you should keep records, it's essential to know exactly how well you are doing at any given time. Now you may *think* that you know how well you are doing, but often it's hard to keep track of all your transactions (don't forget the interest on your account and the dividends). I have a master record which I update every time I buy or sell share, and at any time I know both this year's and my lifetime's outlay, expenditure, turnover and net profit. This is not complicated to do, either using spreadsheet software or a manual record.

WATCH OUT

- Don't believe everything that you read on the Internet.

- Make your own judgement about the ethics of your trading style.

- Cut your losses, don't buy things that you don't understand, don't trade out of habit and do take security seriously. Remember that *nobody* can predict from minute to minute what the markets will do.

- Don't buy shares on a whim, don't get obsessed with online share trading and record everything that you do. Above all, don't give up your day job.

PART THREE

other
information

9

options,
futures and other
incredibly risky bets

Let's be clear. . . most of these financial products really *are* risky and you can lose a great deal of money in a very short time if you don't know what you're doing.

In the UK, online share trading has been available to the masses for relatively no time at all. In that time, the pace of change has been huge, and it can't be long before it's possible to buy a range of other financial products on the web. One sort of financial instrument that has become astoundingly popular over the last few decades is generally referred to as a *derivative product*. There is one huge difference between derivative products and ordinary shares: though, like shares, derivative products have an intrinsic value themselves, that value depends on the value of *something else* (usually a share or an index). This is different from an ordinary share, where the value of a share depends only on how much the share is worth.

There are many sorts of derivative product, and they are traded in huge quantities on exchanges the world over. Some are extremely complicated and will not concern us here, but others are relatively simple and can easily be explained. As far as I am aware, there are currently very few places where it is possible to buy such things online, but it can only be a matter of time before anyone will be able to trade derivative products on the net.

This book is about online share buying and for most of us that's quite risky enough. Nevertheless, in anticipation of this 'new buying opportunity', it's as well to know the details of some of these products, and to understand the potential risks and rewards. Let's be clear right from the start, though: most of these financial products *really are risky* and you can lose a great deal of money in a very short time if you don't know what you're doing.

Options

The rise of options and futures in the financial world has been meteoric. These high-tech products first began to be traded in Chicago in about 1973 and are now worth so much of the total value of many banks that serious worries have been expressed about a possible 'melt-down' of world banking systems if all the debts were simultaneously called in. Options are traded in London by LIFFE (the London International Financial Futures and options Exchange) and if you really want to know what happens there, then arrange a trip: they are only to pleased to welcome visitors.

So what exactly is an option? Before we can understand this, we need to identify the 'underlying'. This is normally just a share (or the value of an index like say the FTSE-100) on which the whole bet (you can call it something fancy if you want to, but basically it's just a bet) will be based. Let's suppose that good old Glaxo Wellcome is our underlying. Then:

- a *call* option gives one the right (but not the obligation) to *buy* a Glaxo Wellcome share at an agreed price E (known as the 'strike price' or just the 'strike') on a given date T (known as the 'expiry').
- a *put* option gives one the right (but not the obligation) to *sell* a Glaxo Wellcome share at an agreed price E (known as the 'strike price' or just the 'strike') on a given date T (known as the 'expiry').

Why should we be interested in doing this? The basic idea is that it's neat to buy things for less than they are really worth and it's also just as neat to sell things for more than they are really worth. So suppose that I have a (call) option to buy Glaxo Wellcome shares for 1850p at some time T in the future, and when that time arrives the shares are *actually* valued at 2000p. Money for jam! I just buy the share for 1850p and sell it again immediately for its real price 2000p, realising an instant profit of 150p. This example shows graphically that if one thinks that a share will rise in value, then one should buy calls.

If, on the other hand, one thinks that times are likely to be hard and that a particular share will go *down* in value, then puts are the thing to buy. The example runs almost the same as the one discussed above, but now we get a chance to sell the share for *more* than it's worth.

That's the upside of options. So where is the risk? Well as you might imagine the right to buy or sell a share at a specific price on a specific date is quite a good thing to have. As you may have guessed by now, this right does not come cheap. The people arrange all this (i.e. who 'write' the option) don't *give* you calls or puts, they *sell* them to you. You pay upfront for the privilege, and herein lies the downside. Let's go back to our previous example. Suppose I paid out some of my hard-earned cash to buy a Glaxo Wellcome call, but when the expiry date T came around, Glaxo Wellcome shares were actually worth *less* than the strike price E. What do I do now? Buying the share for *more* than it's worth would add insult to injury, so all that I can do is to choose not to exercise (as we said above, the option gives you the *right* to exercise – but you don't have to). Tear up the contract! As you can see, it's like tearing up your own money that you previously paid to buy the option.

It's also worth pointing out at this stage that there are actually two sorts of way that the expiry of options can work. All of the options that we have discussed so far are known as European options. These expire on a given date (which we called T), and that's the one and only date when all the profits and losses, winnings and losings, fortunes or bankruptcies are worked out. It's also possible to buy American options. There is only one difference between European and American options, which is that American options can be exercised *at any time* prior to the expiry T. As you might expect, the extra freedom that an American option brings means that American options are generally more expensive than European options. By the way, the terms European and American are sort of historical accidents and imply nothing at all about where the option is being written. European options are traded in the US and American options are traded in Europe. They're just names that signify what sort of expiry arrangements apply.

Space does not permit a much fuller description of options, but basically option writers make a living by selling options for slightly more than they are worth, and then 'hedging' their position so that they can guarantee not to make a loss. Hedging sounds complicated, but it's actually pretty similar to what happens if you go to a small bookmaker and try to put £10,000 on the favourite in the 3.30 at Kempton Park. Since it is a small place, the bookie will have to 'lay off' your bet before he can risk accepting it. The laying off procedure consists of the bookie sending some of his minions to bet on the favourite at other betting shops. That way he probably wins whatever happens. It is rare for option writers not to be hedged. If this does happen, then the writer is said to have written a 'naked option' or to have 'taken a naked position'.

People who *buy* options may be doing so for purposes of pure speculation. If they are pension funds and the like, however, they may also be guarding themselves against unwanted short-term movements in the share price. In most option transactions, no shares are actually bought or sold; at expiry one simply settles up with the writer. Options can also be actively traded themselves. For example, if you buy a call option and the price of the underlying rises rapidly then clearly the call that you hold is worth more now than when you originally bought it. Rather than hanging on to it until expiry, you might sell it on to somebody else and make your profit straight away without having to worry whether or not things will still all be hunky dory at expiry.

Only the most basic sort of option (usually referred to as a 'vanilla' – i.e. a standard flavour) has been described above, but for those who want to indulge in ever more exotic bets there are almost as many different types of option as there are shares. Some people trade Asian, Barrier, Passport and Shout options and others trade Ladder, Parisian, Russian and Stop-loss options. There are hundreds of others too. It's also worth pointing out that if you really crave some novelty in your options trading, then not only are there a great many different ways of working out the payoff, but there is also an ever-increasing variety of strange underlying indices that you can bet on. One of the most bizarre of these sidelines is the business of 'weather options'. Yes, that's right: the underlying is not a share or a financial index, but the amount of rain that falls each day, the number of sunshine hours, or the average humidity. You can find out all about weather options on **www.weatherderivs.com** if you're sceptical, but people really *do* trade things like this (especially if they're fleece jacket manufacturers, for example, who want to hedge themselves against poor sales in a warm winter).

The gearing is huge

So that you can appreciate the huge 'gearing' that's inevitably involved in buying options, let's consider what might happen if a relative bequeathed you £1000, which you decide to invest. We might as well spend the lot on our example company Glaxo Wellcome. For definiteness, we'll assume that it's Thursday, 24 February 2000 and ignore all dealing charges and spreads.

Looking in the *Financial Times*, we see that Glaxo's price is currently 1482p. We take a bullish view and think that the shares will rise; we must now decide

FIG. 9.1. Weather options really do exist!

whether to blow the inheritance buying shares or call options. A few pages on in the *Financial Times*, we find the LIFFE page, and note that May calls on Glaxo with a strike price of 1600p are available for a mere 78p. Here are our choices.

■ Spend the £1000 on Glaxo shares. We buy at 1482p and therefore get 67 shares (we'll ignore fractions of shares and other such minutiae).

■ Spend the £1000 on May expiry Glaxo calls with a strike of 1600p. Since each call costs 78p, our thousand pounds buys us 1282 calls.

So what happened at expiry? Glaxo actually performed rather well. When the option expired on the third Friday in May the share price had risen to 1986p. Here's what would have happened to each of our strategies:

Strategy 1: sell 67 shares at 1986p = £1331. Profit = £331 (+33 per cent)

Strategy 2: sell 1282 options each for the difference between the current price and the strike (which is 1986p−1600p = 386p) = £4949. Profit = £3949 (+295 per cent)

Whatever we did we made a nice profit, but the profit from buying options was *over ten times larger* than that from buying the shares. Before we get too carried away though, let's ponder for a second to consider what would have happened if, on the third Friday of May Glaxo shares had risen, but only say to 1550p. The sums look horribly different now:

Strategy 1: sell 67 shares at 1550p = £1039. Profit = £39 (+4 per cent)

Strategy 2: price is less than strike; option expires worthless = £0. Profit = −£1000 (−100 per cent)

In this case, using the inheritance to buy shares has actually gained us a little, but using it to buy options has blown it completely. As we said; the gearing is huge.

But how do they work out how much options cost?

Option writers soon realised that if they wanted to make a living from selling options and hedging them then it was clear that accurate valuation methods were absolutely essential. Nevertheless the tricky question of how to determine the fair value of even a European vanilla option unanswered for many years. Oh sure, there were complicated and rather unsuccessful mathematical theories, but the market tended to use its own rules of thumb and nobody really knew what to do. Then three economathematicians (Fischer Black, Robert Merton and Myron Scholes) came up with a really cunning idea, which eventually won Merton and Scholes (sadly Black had died by then) the 1997 Nobel prize for Economics. It's not often possible to explain a Nobel-prize winning idea in a few lines, but let's have a go anyway: the basis of what is now known as the Black-Scholes model for option pricing may be stated in the following statements.

■ The stock market moves like a random walk.

■ If options cost too much to buy then nobody would buy them: they would put their money in the bank instead – if options were too cheap then all the banks would go bust and everybody would only ever buy options. Somewhere in between lies the 'fair value' of an option.

■ By constructing a portfolio consisting one of option and *a cunningly chosen* (possibly negative) number of the underlying stock it is possible to eliminate risk completely ('perfect hedging').

The above is a crude and very horrible bastardisation of what the theory actually says, but for our purposes it'll be sufficient. The bottom line is that with quite a lot of mathematical fooling around, it's possible to show that the 'fair value' V of an option satisfies the equation

$$\frac{\partial V}{\partial t} + \frac{1}{2}\sigma^2 S^2 \frac{\partial^2 V}{\partial S^2} + rS\frac{\partial V}{\partial S} - rV = 0.$$

Yikes! a real mathematical equation! Option writers understand how to solve this equation to determine V. The only thing that should be of any interest to you is what the equation (and therefore the fair value of an option) depends on. Steeling ourselves to look at the equation again, we see that it depends on:

- t (the time to expiry);
- S (the price of the underlying);
- σ (the volatility of the underlying);
- r (the interest rate).

These quantities are therefore the things that you will be wanting to keep track of if you ever get into the business of trading options.

It won't be long before a good deal of amateur investors trade options online. If you decide to start doing it yourself then you're going to have a good deal of fun and you could also make yourself large sums of money, but for goodness' sake beware and make sure that you know *exactly* what you are getting into before you make your first trade.

Futures

People may try to blind you with science about futures, but there's really only one difference between a future and an option: with a future you *must* exercise. Futures are therefore just like puts and calls, but the right to decide to tear the contract up if things are not going your way is no longer present.

As you might imagine, this makes futures even more dramatically risky than options and frankly you'd be well advised against even thinking of dabbling in them unless you have considerable experience in trading derivative products.

Although superficially (and mathematically as well) options and futures are very similar, there are some major differences in the *modus operandi* for trading futures. First, while options are usually only traded on share and index prices, futures can be bought on a range of commodities too. Every day all over the world futures are bought and sold on silver, heating oil, lumber, Euros, pork bellies, sugar, hogs and oats. Second, when you buy a future there is no 'upfront' payment like in an options contract. If you think that the underlying will rise in price, you take a 'long' (i.e. buy) position, and if you think that the price will fall you take a 'short' (i.e. sell) position. Every so often (maybe at the end of each trading day) the positions are tallied up and your account balance increases or decreases.

In the US, real time online futures are commonplace. Most deals are traded on margin, and huge amounts are regularly won or lost on the smallest of movements in the values of commodities and indices. If you're so desperate to start playing this hugely risky game that you can't wait for the UK to catch up, then of course you could open a US account. In the UK, however, the current position is that few (if any) e-brokers provide a futures service (although see, for example **www.mandirect.co.uk**). This situation is bound to change soon.

The Connection with Spread Betting

Actually, the statement that it's almost impossible to buy options or futures on the Internet at the moment is not quite true, because it's possible to buy *spread bets* at a number of recently established sites. (See chapter 10 for details.)

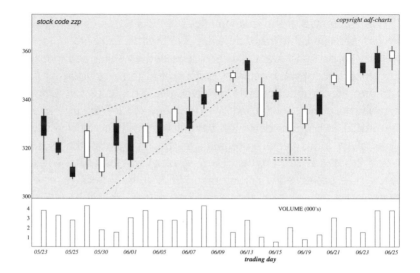

FIG. 9.2. Candlestick charts: the sort of games that online futures traders play

Spread betting on the net started as a novel way of having a flutter on sporting events, and is probably most easily explained in terms of a sport. Since the first sport on which spread bets were offered was cricket, this is the example that we'll examine.

Picture the scene: it's a sunny day at Lords' and Australia have won the toss and chosen to bat. How many do we think that Australia will make in their first innings? The wicket is good and as usual, we expect to see our bowling attack caned all over the park by the Australians. So let's guess at about 400. Now it's down to the bookies to put our money where our mouth is, and we see that they are advertising 'Aus. 1st Innings: 340–355: £1 a run'.

The range 340–355 is known as the 'spread'. If we think that Australia will make 400 then we *buy the spread at 355* (since this is the top of the spread). Nine hours later, a toiling England attack finally takes the last wicket and Australia are all out for 412. How does the bet work now? By buying the spread we effectively backed Australia to make over 355. Actually, they made 57 runs more than this. We bought the spread at £1 a run, so the bet makes us £57.

What would have happened if (by some miracle) Australia had been skittled out for 120? Well now things are not so good. We bought the spread at 355, and the difference between 355 and 120 is 235. At £1 a run, we now owe the bookies £235! Of course, if we'd *sold the spread* instead, then we'd have made the difference between the bottom of the spread and the final score, viz 340 120 = £220 profit.

As you can see, spread betting is very risky. It's also essentially *exactly the same* as a future. As you can also see, spread bets can be placed on anything that has a value. Like, for example, shares and indices. There are a number of sites where you can place spread bets on share prices. At **www.cantorindex.com**, for example, Cantor Fitzgerald (one of America's biggest brokers) allows you to bet on the FTSE-100, The DOW Jones, the NASDAQ and the Nikkei as well as on blue chip shares on the London Stock Exchange. Of course, the broker's 'edge' is set entirely by the spread: since no shares are ever bought or sold there is no stamp duty and no commission. You can register free, but (as you might have guessed) before you open an account you have to prove that you can pay if you lose.

Spread betting on shares is here now in the UK for you to enjoy online and in real time. Large amounts of money can be won or lost in a short time though, and because of this spread betting undoubtedly deserves its place in our 'incredibly risky' class of online share dealing opportunities. You have been warned.

Warrants

Another derivative contract that is similar to an option is a *warrant*. Warrants are basically call options issued by a company on its own equity. They're not quite the same as vanilla calls though because when the holder of a warrant exercises it the company issues *new* stock to the warrant holder, whereas the exerciser of a traded option receives stock that is already 'in circulation'. Another major difference between options and warrants is the lifespan of the contract: typical warrants last for five years or more. Warrants can normally be exercised at any time after some initial waiting period.

It's hard to find a website where warrants may be traded online and in real time, but it can only be a matter of time before such sites start to spring up. Like options, they are risky (for the same reasons). The leverage is terrific and small changes in the share price of the underlying can lead to massive swings in the warrant value. You can easily make large sums of money for a relatively small outlay, but by the same token you can easily lose *all* of your investment. For experienced gamblers only.

Convertible Bonds

Convertible Bonds (CBs) are another derivative product which are sort of half way between bonds and warrants. They pay coupons (which are just a fancy name for dividends paid on bonds) and pay out like a standard bond at maturity, but they can be converted into stock before expiry if the holder wishes. Once conversion takes place, no more coupons are payable. Since exercise can take place at any time, CBs are in many ways similar to American options; the main idea is that if the stock price is low then the holder does not convert and takes the coupons, but if the stock price is high then the holder forgets about the coupons and converts. Just like warrants and options, CBs are very risky for amateur investors to buy. There's little doubt though that it will be possible to buy them online soon.

Short Selling

As well as derivative products, there are a number of other sorts of ways of gambling on the markets. One is 'selling short'. Short selling is basically the process of selling shares that you don't own. When they first hear of this, most people are a bit shocked and some even assume that this is illegal, but short selling is a well-established practice in the City which is crucial in most hedging strategies.

The simplest way to understand short selling is to think of it as buying a negative number of shares. If you think that a share is going to go up in value, you buy a positive number. If you think that it's going to go down, you buy a negative number. If it *does* actually go down, then hooray: the shares that you 'borrowed' to sell (since you didn't actually own any) can be bought back (for a lower price than you sold them for) to be repatriated to the owner.

In reality, this is almost exactly what happens when a broker short sells a share for somebody. The broker simply 'borrows' the share from someone who owns it, and later, when you buy it back, the broker 'unborrows' it. Most of the time the original holder of the share never even knows that it has been sold!

There is one slight complication: if a dividend is due then the unknowing asset holder who the share has been borrowed from is not going to be too pleased if he or she suddenly stops receiving dividends. In this case, it is up to the short seller to repay the dividend to the original holder of the share.

Before you rush out to try this new game, be warned: short selling is risky. Your losses can be unlimited and the dealing charges can be high. If you really want to dabble, then there are plenty of opportunities to have a dry run first with an imaginary portfolio (try, for example, **www.uk-invest.com**).

As yet, there seem to be no UK websites where you can sell short. This is because currently execution-only online brokers will only allow you to sell stock that is held in your nominee account and will not lend you stock. Presumably it can only be a matter of time before it's possible to do this; for the present though, if you are desperate there are a number of ways of simulating a short sale. One way of doing this is via spread bets, and short sales may also be simulated by buying contracts-for-difference (see below). Of course, if you're really desperate to short a few stocks then as usual you could always consider opening up a US account (see, for example **www.investin.co.uk**).

Contracts-For-Difference

Here's a sneaky idea: suppose you bought *pretend shares* instead of real shares. Then since you're not actually buying anything real at all, there's no stamp duty to pay. Even better, since the person who you pretend to buy them off doesn't actually have to do anything, there should be little or no commission to pay! This cunning plan is the basic idea behind contracts for-difference (CFDs).

Buying or selling a share (or an index value) using a CFD is often likened to borrowing money from the bank to buy shares. The buyer needs no capital upfront and is able to profit from returns on the share, but has to pay the bank for the loan. Normally the way it works is that clients have to deposit a certain percentage (say 20 per cent) of the total stock price to buy it. If the position is closed before the end of trading then there is no finance charge due on the loan: if the position is carried overnight then a fee will normally need to be paid.

This amounts to instant commission-free and stamp-duty free trading on margin, and is a very interesting idea. Unlike short selling, warrants, CBs and the rest, CFDs can be traded online *now*. You can find out more about online CFDs at (for example) **www.cmcplc.com** but if you do decide to trade online this way be absolutely sure that you fully understand what's going on and how much it will cost you to keep a position open, and remember: pretend shares do not carry any dividends.

Do You Feel Lucky?

It's not a very bold prediction to state that in a year or two many people in the UK will be trading all of the financial products described above online and in real time. Most amateur online share traders are relatively conservative by nature and tend to regard the level of risk involved in standard share trading as quite large enough for their taste. For this reason it may be a while before the real time online options and futures market really takes off.

Signs are already visible however that there is a UK market for derivative products and other highly geared forms of trading. Online brokers E*trade, DLJ Direct and T.D. Waterhouse are all set to offer online margin trading late in 2000, and while this may suit some investors, the generally higher commissions and stamp duty that must be paid in the UK make speculation of this type less desirable than in the US.

Whatever you do, if you eventually get into online derivative product trading *be careful* and go into it with your eyes open.

DERIVATIVE PRODUCTS

- Derivative products are *much more risky* than shares and if things go wrong you can lose a great deal of money – fast.

- Currently there are very few sites where options and futures may be traded online, but this state of affairs is *strictly temporary*.

- Don't even consider online trading in options, futures and their relatives unless you are an experienced online share trader.

- If you do decide to trade derivative products make absolutely sure that you know every detail and intricacy of the type of contract that you enter into.

where to find it

All information is good information and all financial information will gradually help you to build up your master plan.

This chapter tells you where to find online trading sites. I have tried to include sites that have provided consistently good service and are periodically updated and regularly reachable. No doubt you'll find many more. A list of further reading is also provided (see page 259).

Websites Providing Online Share Trading Services

- **www.barclays-stockbrokers.co.uk** will give most online investors what they want; a low minimum commission, an easy-to-use site and guaranteed security. It's carefully organised too, and new users are well catered for. Worth a visit.

- **www.dijdirect.co.uk** is a really attractive site with great demos and a large amount of helpfully set out information. If you trade with them you get real time stock quotes (500 for starters and 100 more for each trade: a good idea) and there are extensive charting facilities. There's all the usual information on your portfolio and trading account and commissions are low. Recommended.

- **www.cmcplc.com** is not so much an online share trading service as an online CFD (Contracts-For-Difference) service (see chapter 9). This amounts to a crafty dodge where trading is on margin and no shares are ever actually bought or sold; all transactions are therefore theoretically both commission-free and stamp-duty free. It's worth finding out *lots* about deals like this before giving them a try but this site will tell you nearly everything that you need know.

- **www.etrade.co.uk** gets most people's vote as being one of the best online brokers around. They pay a reasonable rate of interest on balances of over £1000, their security is up to scratch, they have a free telephone helpline and generally provide a most satisfactory service. Highly recommended.

- **www.halifax-online.co.uk** has recently been updated and improved – the result is an interesting and informative site. All the information that you need to be able to understand what's what is neatly laid out, and if you're not planning on trading very often then this could be the site for you.

- **www.idealing.com** is a new online trading service that looks likely to cause a commission war. The site comes in 'any flavour you like as long as it's vanilla' (their words) so don't expect any pretty HTML. It also carries no charting facilities (though as they point out, these are available at many other free sites). In fact the only thing that's *not* plain about the site is the commission: £10 per trade for *any trade*. That's a fraction of what anybody else charges.

- **www.iii.co.uk** offers a huge range of products as well as online trading. These include online banking, insurance, ISAs and mortgages. If you register (free, and done in a moment) then you can read about their online share dealing service.

- **schwab-worldwide.com/europe** is a very well-known online share trading service. The site is clear, attractive and easy to navigate. Schwab also usually offer various perks like free trading for the first 30 days after you open your account. The trading demo is absolutely the best that there is on the web. You can also trade after-hours on the NASDAQ. Highly recommended.

- **www.share.co.uk** is 'the share centre'. After opening an account in the usual way you can buy and sell online; the stated objective of the site is 'to make share ownership easy and affordable for everyone'. One of the key selling points of the site is the heavily advertised minimum commission of just £2.50. A solid site, it's easy to navigate and also carries lots of other information on things like ISAs.

- **www.sharepeople.com** is one of the newer sites. It claims to 'bring shares and people together' and looking at its user-friendly site it's not hard to see why. You can manage real or imaginary portfolios of stocks on the London Stock Exchange, AIM, NYSE and NASDAQ and there are all sorts of little extras like a webcam of their office and their 'stay-alert' service which automatically e-mails or pages you when any of your shares hit pre-specified limits. Intensively advertised on television, this might well be just what you're looking for.

- **www.stocktrade.co.uk** struck me as a nicely set out site which claims to have launched its online service as far back as 1996. I particularly liked the FAQ section (the answers were brief and clear – no messing around). There's also a helpful trading demo. You should certainly check this site out when you're looking for an e-broker.

- **www.xest.com** has greatly benefited from a recent upgrade. The online share trading service offers some very competitive commission and interest rates. Unlike some other e-brokers, limit buying is also allowed on a 'fill-or-kill' basis.

Sites with Information and Other Things

- **www.bankruptcy.co.uk** You won't need this, will you? It's a real site though.

- **www.digitallook.co.uk/pages/tips_watcher.html** includes all the current tips from the Sunday (and sometimes other) papers. Such tips are often unreliable, but just the same shares sometimes move because of them.

- **www.epo.com** is a site that deals with new issues in the form of 'electronic public offerings'. For more details, see chapter 7.

- **www.europeaninvestor.com** is a nicely laid out site with lots of useful features which concentrates particularly on the European rather than just the British scene. It's free to register, and once you have done so a number of portfolio tracking facilities are available. Real time quotes are also offered and there's a useful online broker comparison section.

- **www.eye4money.com** is an interesting site that has been specifically set up to allow investors to practice online share dealing before risking real money. Participants get a sum of £100,000 'virtual capital' to invest over a period of six weeks and there are prizes for the best performers. Good for nervous beginners.

- **www.find.co.uk** contains no specific financial information itself, but is a directory of online financial resources. Whatever sort of financial help or data you want, you'll probably find the right URL here. Definitely a must-bookmark site.

- **www.fool.co.uk** is the famous 'Motley Fool' site. Its stated aim is to 'amuse, educate and enrich individuals in search of the truth'. This objective is accomplished in the most humorous fashion. The site contains masses and masses of information which is presented in an easily accessible and highly amusing manner. The 'fool's eye view' is particularly well worth reading. A fantastic and useful site: don't miss it.

- **www.financial-freebies.com** has a range of free things that you can download to both help and entertain you. Most are software demos or example copies of magazines. Some are free tip sheets which, as usual, should be treated with caution. Nevertheless, some fun things are to be had here.

- **www.freeware.co.uk** is not the best site in the world for detailed financial information, but it does have one great feature: the downloadable tickerboo desktop stock ticker.

- **www.ft.com** turns out to be exactly the sort of website that you might expect from the *Financial Times*. The coverage is huge, the sheer amount of data that can be accessed is massive, and there are as many different parts to the site as you could ever wish for. An essential web resource.

- **www.ftyourmoney.com** has a good portfolio tracker and some neat calculators. It's related to the FT site but promises more on personal finance issues 'for people that don't spend most of their time thinking about money'.

- **www.gomez.com** is a 'ratings' site that includes pages on online brokers. Here you can find how all the competing services measure up to each other. The only problem is that there are also other ratings sites which rank online brokers and agreement is by no means universal. So before accepting their word as final, you should look at some of the other 'comparison' sites.

- **www.hemscott.net** is a great site for all sorts of information. Virtually any financial data that you require can be obtained here, and it's all free. The site is very deep and is constantly updated – very highly recommended.

- **www.igindex.co.uk** is not an online share broker, but an online financial betting site offering a range of spread betting facilities with all the usual advantages (such as the fact that no tax or stamp duty is payable) and all the usual disadvantages (it's gruesomely risky). You can place bets online in real time 24 hours a day, and the site includes a range of useful charting facilities. If you're brave enough to be interested, have a go at their rather nifty demo.

- **www.issuesdirect.com** is a crucial site to know about if you want to become involved in flotations and new issues. For fuller details, see chapter 7.

- **www.londonstockexchange.com** has a very cool webcam. As well as this eye candy, it is a very neat and well-organised site which has masses of information about the London Stock Exchange, AIM, techMARK, trading and all the rest of it. Highly recommended.

- **www.marketeye.co.uk** is one of my particular favourites: there is a no-registration service and a pay-to-use service, but the free registration part of the site provides so much useful information on current prices, biggest movers of the day, share price charts (downloadable) and many, many other things that it's quite adequate for most purposes.

- **www.moneyworld.co.uk** is a great-looking site with a very convenient portfolio-tracking service. If you take advantage of the free registration service then you'll receive a free e-mail newsletter which has all sorts of advice about share dealing and other online investments. The charting section of the site is also particularly good (should you want to indulge in this).

- **www.nothing-ventured.com** is run by e-brokers Durlacher and deals with online investing in new issues: for further details see chapter 7. The companies concerned are normally very small and speculative and are certainly not for the faint-hearted.

- **www.thisismoney.com** describes itself as a 'personal finance adviser from the *Daily Mail*, *Mail on Sunday* and *Evening Standard*'. It includes a nice Sunday papers' share tips round up and a helpful introductory section on online share dealing.

- **www.uk-invest.com** A fantastically useful site with a great deal of relevant information. Particularly good coverage of Directors' dealings, news briefings, and what 'experts' are tipping which share, and why. Also offers share club, portfolio services and a great deal more besides.

■ **uk.finance.yahoo.com** is a really neat site that contains loads of information on all sorts of share-related matters. One of the best things about this site is that, after you've registered (free), you can set up your own portfolio and have instant access to slightly delayed share prices. Other sites offer this too, but the yahoo service is undoubtedly one of the quickest and most convenient such services. Check it out.

Do You Remember That Stuff *Paper*?

You should obtain information from as many different sources as you can. All information is good information and all financial information will gradually help you build up your master plan. All I can safely do therefore is to list some books and publications that I've read, enjoyed, found provocative and/or useful, and recommend that you read them too.

■ *Beating The Dow* (Michael O'Higgins, Harperbusiness, reprinted 2000). This has deservedly become the classic book on the tactic of picking your buys by their dividend yield. Although it's getting on a bit by now, most of it still makes sound sense and you should add this to your 'must read sometime' list.

■ *Beating The Street* (Peter Lynch, Fireside, 1994). Peter Lynch achieved something like cult status in the US during the 1980s when his legendary Magellan fund regularly trounced the opposition. How did he pick his stocks and what were his tactics? Read this well-written book to find out.

- *Beyond the Zulu Principle* (Jim Slater, Orion, 1996). If growth shares are what grabs you, then this and its predecessor *The Zulu Principle* are the classic books on how to spot them, when to buy them, and when to sell them (at a huge profit of course). Jim Slater has had a slightly chequered career but he's still probably forgotten more about what make companies do well than most of us will ever know. Essential reading.

- *Company REFS* (Hemmington Scott, published monthly in paper and as a CD). This is the Rolls-Royce of company data publications. It boasts massively detailed coverage of every UK company and includes complete brokers' forecasts and a set of very useful consolidated tables which list things like companies with the lowest PEGs, highest ROCE, etc. The only problem is the price, which at almost £300 for a quarterly subscription is pretty steep. If you can afford it though this is a fantastic source of data.

- *The Complete Idiot's Guide To Online Investing* (Douglas Gerlach, QUE, 1999). This includes a little information on online share trading but covers all sorts of online trading from mutual funds to futures. It also seems to be aimed mainly at the US investor. Well worth a read, but don't expect advanced stockpicking advice.

- *Day Trade Online* (Christopher A. Farrell, John Wiley & Sons Ltd, 1999). You've been warned before about day trading, but you just won't listen, will you? If you really *have* to consider giving up your job to be a day trader then at least read this book: it's encouragingly realistic and gives an accurate account of the downside of day trading as well as the benefits.

- *Derivatives* (Paul Wilmott, John Wiley & Sons Ltd, 1998). You want to know how to do the sums involved in derivative products properly? This gargantuan (but relatively cheap) epic is the place to look in. Be warned though: there's mathematics a-plenty and it's not a cosy bedtime read.

- *Electronic Day Trading 101* (Sunny J. Harris, John Wiley & Sons Ltd, 1999). So you want to use the Internet to be a day trader, huh? You want to buy and sell risky shares all day long and never leave a position open overnight? This book will tell you all that you need to know about day trading; cynics however will say that all you need to know about day trading is that 80 per cent of day traders make a loss. Your choice.

- The *Financial Times* (especially on Saturday). In spite of its somewhat conservative reputation the *FT* has a lot to offer and you should read it regularly. The Saturday edition contains full business coverage, high quality personal investment section and good features.

- *Getting Started in Futures* (Todd Lofton, John Wiley & Sons Ltd, 1997). This is the book that you must read if you're tempted to try your hand at the awesomely risky game of online futures trading. It'll show you what you can expect to happen and teach you the basics of margin trading, candlestick charts, and all the rest of it.

- *How I Trade For A Living* (Gary Smith, B.T., John Wiley & Sons Ltd, 2000). A very US-oriented book which contains the story of how the author turned a position of virtual bankruptcy into loads of money. As the blurb for the book says: 'What did he discover on that fateful day in 1985?'. If you really want to know then buy this book. Also contains some useful views on US markets and the way that they move.

- *How To Invest In Sports Shares* (Benjamin Cooper & Andrew McHaltie, B.T., Batsford Ltd, 1997). This book covers one of the more esoteric pleasures, that of buying shares in football clubs and other related interests. If online football is your thing, then you should check it out as niche areas like this play to a certain extent by their own sets of rules.

- *How To Make A Killing In the Share Jungle* (Michael Walters, Rushmere Wynne Ltd, 1996). This is a nice introductory book which will tell you all that you need to know about the basics of the markets and how they move. There's nothing about online trading (which was not even a glint in the eye of the Internet when the book was written) but there is an especially good section at the end of the book which gives candid advice on some of the City's big players.

- *How To Read The Financial Pages* (Michael Brett, Century Business Ltd, 1995). Slightly dated, slightly simple-minded, but great for brushing up on all those definitions and concepts that you haven't quite got around to mastering yet. Highly recommended for beginners.

- *Investors Chronicle Magazine* (published weekly). This is probably the best and most informative of the weekly magazines that you can buy. With a well-established and solid reputation, it adopts a somewhat downbeat approach, but rarely gets it wrong. Read the analysis carefully and it can only add to your share-valuation arsenal.

- *The Motley Fool Guide To Online Investing* (Nigel Roberts and David Berger, Boxtree, 2000). This slim paperback is a cheap way of learning the basics of online investment. It doesn't include much information on the tactics of online share buying and selling but is still a good read.

- *The Motley Fool UK Investment Guide* (David Berger *et al.*, Boxtree, 1998). This witty and well-informed book will tell you a great deal of what you need to know about investment in the UK and also tell you how to spot 'obviously great investments' and even 'less obvious obviously good investments'. Highly recommended.

- *Net Benefit: Guaranteed Electronic Markets – The Ultimate Potential of Online Trade* (Wingham Rowan, Macmillan Business, 1999). Bored with price charts? Unimpressed with the vagaries of market movements? Then you could do worse than to read this highly original view on new ways of thinking about our economic and social future.

- *Net-Trading* (Alpesh B. Patel, ft.com, 2000). An extremely interesting book which is packed with information. Some is relevant to British online traders but the accent is unmistakably American and the book is really aimed at day traders. There is a great deal of coverage of technical analysis (or as we call it in the UK, charting) which will show you the details of some of the crazy schemes that are used to try to predict short-term share price movements. Coverage of derivatives trading is also very good.

- *Shares Magazine* (published weekly). A relatively new venture: if *Investors Chronicle* is the BMW of share magazines, then *Shares Magazine* is a Ford Escort. Has plenty of useful information though and a very readable website at **www.sharesmagazine.com**. Just don't take all of the tips too seriously.

- *The UK Guide To Online Investing* (Michael Scott, McGraw-Hill, 2000). This covers every sort of online investing that you might ever want to get involved with. The coverage of online share buying is fairly brief, but it also includes sections on ISAs, unit and investment trusts and bank accounts. It also contains more screen grabs than any other book that I have read.

- *The Warren Buffett Way* (Robert G. Hagstrom Jr, John Wiley & Sons Ltd, 1995). Saying that this Buffett chap does quite well shares-wise is a bit like saying that Ghengis Khan could be a mite tetchy sometimes. If you want to know how the all-time champion of the shares game thinks and acts and what makes him buy and sell, then this is the book for you.

financial glossary

Act analy (activity analysis): this shows what the company does and how and where it makes its money. For example, it'll tell you things like the fact that Glaxo Wellcome make 28 per cent of their profit in Europe, 39 per cent in the US and the other third in the rest of the world. It should also tell you that their profit is in the following proportions: 27 per cent (respiratory), 17 per cent (viral infections), 15 per cent (central nervous system disorders), 10 per cent (gastro-intestinal) and 31 per cent in other areas.

Beta rel (beta relative): measures relative volatility. The market's volatility is one, so shares with a Beta greater than one tend to move more violently than the market while those with a Beta less than one are less volatile than the market in general.

Cover, or Div cover (dividend cover): is a measure of how 'safe' the dividend is. This figure attempts to assess the extent to which the company's earnings can pay the dividend. To calculate it, divide EPS by the net dividend per share. Covers of 3 or 4 give one a nice warm feeling inside, but do not prove much. Low covers mean more, for if there has to be a cut in the dividend this may have severe consequences for the share price.

CR (current ratio): this is found by dividing the current assets of a business by its current liabilities, and is similar to the quick ratio explained below. A current ratio in excess of about 1.5 is usually a sign of a company that has some financial clout; the actual numbers involved are somewhat sector-dependent though and should be checked for each company against suitable sector comparators.

Div est (dividend estimate): is an informed guess made by averaging the dividends that are predicted by various brokers for the next year or two years. The brokers usually know about the company's future order book, expected profits and planned expansion and in this sense the forecast is usually quite accurate (especially if more than just one or two brokers are involved). Watch out for changes though: a suddenly revised dividend forecast can spell either good news or impending disaster.

Dir holdings (directors' shareholdings): show how many shares each of the main directors holds. This gives one an idea of how much they have 'bought into' their own business and, more importantly, allows one to calculate how significant directors' share purchases might be.

DY (dividend yield): to determine this, divide the gross dividend per share by the latest share price and multiply by 100 to get a percentage. A high yield may mean that the company is exceptionally generous to its shareholders. Far more often though the yield is high because the share price is low. One popular theory is that this means that the markets have over-reacted and the share is therefore a good recovery buy.

EPS (earnings per share): is a key financial statistic. Essentially, it's worked out by dividing the company's total earnings by the number of shares in circulation. This simple definition hides a web of complexity, however, most of which arises from the knotty problem of exactly how one defines 'earnings'. The subtleties are probably not worth bothering about: the important thing is that a rising EPS is obviously a good thing.

FRS3 (Financial Reporting Standard 3): are the conventions that are supposed to be used to work out key financial statistics like EPS. FRS3 now governs the presentation of all profit and loss accounts, but there are those who feel that the figures produced by this standard are opaque and hard to interpret and as a result other methods of working out the figures have also evolved. This is why you sometimes see two or even three different figures quoted for EPS.

Gear (gearing): tells you how much the company owes. To determine it, (there are some complications but these need not concern us here) divide the borrowings by the shareholders' funds and express the result as a percentage. Obviously cash-rich companies (with low, or even negative gearing) are generally at an advantage compared to companies with excessive borrowing which may be prey to liquidity crises or sensitive to interest rate changes. Gearing of over 50 per cent is generally a cause for concern unless there is a logical explanation.

GR (growth rate): measures how fast a company is expanding. To find the growth rate of a company for a given period, subtract the previous EPS from the EPS for the period in question and divide the whole lot by the previous EPS. Multiplying by 100 now gives the growth rate as a percentage. Obviously negative GR is possible if EPS has decreased. Frequently the most useful incarnation of growth rate is when it is based on *prospective* EPS and so 'foresees the future'.

IIMR (IIMR figures): are nothing to make a fuss about. The IIMR (Institute of Investment Management and Research) feel that the latest official rules for working out EPS have made Earnings Per Share a less valuable statistic than it should be. They have therefore set out their own guidelines for calculating EPS and other figures. IIMR and FRS3 are thus different ways of calculating what is supposed to be the same financial statistic.

IND (index): tells you what 'division' a share is in. The 100 largest companies (by market capitalisation) make up the FTSE-100. These are the heavyweights, which are followed in punching power by the FTSE Mid-250 index, the FTSE Smallcap index, and finally the featherweight FTSE Fledgling index.

Ind changes (index promotion/demotion candidates): there are essentially four 'divisions' (in order of importance, the FTSE-100, FTSE Mid-250, FTSE Smallcap and FTSE Fledgling) and every three months or so companies whose market cap has risen or fallen sufficiently are respectively promoted or relegated. Promotion to the FTSE-100 is particularly important as all the tracker funds then have to buy the shares so that they can accurately reflect the FTSE-100's performance. By the same token a recently relegated poor performer is likely to suffer temporarily as the tracker funds sell.

Int cover (interest cover): tells you how easy it is for a company to carry on paying off their debts. It is worked out by dividing the company's profits (before tax) by their annual gross interest charge. You don't need to be a genius to see that if this ratio drops to one, then disaster may follow. A low or reducing value of interest cover is therefore an obvious black mark against the future prospects of a company.

Key dates (key dates in the financial year): can be quite important when you come to make your final 'buy' or 'sell' decision. All companies run their year as *they* wish and thus different outfits report at different times. Normally there are seven 'key dates', consisting of the final ex-div date, the interim ex-div date, the year end, the preliminary results date, the annual report date, the AGM date and the final results date.

LSE (London Stock Exchange): the UK's leading stock exchange. It can trace its roots as far back as 1553, though the name 'The Stock Exchange' was not assumed until 1773.

MAR (margin): may be worked out by dividing the profit by the turnover. It provides a measure of how efficiently sales are being turned into profit, but is something of a double-edged sword. On the face of it, large margins are good. Large margins invite competition though and a firm with large margins may find itself being priced out of the market. Small margins are normally bad, as they make the profit and therefore the share price sensitive to very small changes in market conditions.

Market cap (market capitalisation): to work this out, simply multiply the number of shares in circulation by the current share price. The market cap of a company thus gives you an instant idea of the size and standing of a company.

NMS (normal market size): gives an idea of the normal size of trade in the stock and therefore allow one to estimate its liquidity. The lowest NMS band is 500, which indicates an average trade of 0–667 shares; the highest is 200,000 which corresponds to an average share trade of more than 160,000. In general, the highest the NMS band, the more market makers will deal in the stock. It therefore follows that shares of small companies have a small NMS and this often points to large spreads.

NormEPS (normalised earnings per share): is very similar to EPS but is normally based on broker forecasts for time periods in the future. There are various complicated rules for deciding what can and what cannot be included in earnings, but the figure is worked out so as to try to reflect the underlying trading position of the company.

NYSE (New York Stock Exchange): is the biggest exchange in the world. Listing over 3,000 companies, it started trading under its current name on 29 January 1863, having been established in May 1792 by 24 New York brokers.

PBV (price to book value): this is obtained by dividing the share price of a company by its net asset value per share. For the calculation of PBV *everything* is included as an asset. This may be a problem as it's normally very hard to estimate how much a patent or a licence is really worth. Notwithstanding this major caveat, a low PBV is usually regarded as a good thing.

PCF (price to cash flow ratio): is found by dividing the company's market cap by the cash flow. Here a problem arises: what exactly do we mean by cash flow? In its simplest form, cash flow consists of profits plus items that don't cost anything (like depreciation), but the definition can get much more complicated. The key thing as far as PCF is concerned is that it indicates how much cash flow you are buying per share. If PCF is high (say much higher than the PER) then this can spell danger as the company may be cash-short. If, on the other hand PCF is low, then this is usually regarded as a point in the share's favour.

PEG (price/earnings growth ratio): is calculated by dividing the prospective PER for the next year by the prospective growth rate for the next year. A low PEG value (under 1 say) is therefore a good indicator of prospective growth and value. The PEG is a multidimensional measure of a company's prospects: for further details, see chapter 6.

PER (price/earnings ratio): provides potential investors with an instant insight into the sort of company that there are considering putting their money into. PER is calculated by dividing the current share price by EPS. One way of thinking about PER is that it's a measure of how much you're being asked to pay for future profits. A high PER is risky as even a small setback can severely affect the share price: a low PER may be indicative of a company where not a lot is happening. Recovery stocks often have high PERs when they are at the bottom of their cycle. An average PER 'used to be' about 20, but Internet stock insanity has seen companies trading with PERs in the hundreds and even the thousands.

Personnel (personnel changes): might not seem like such a big deal, but are worth keeping track of. A high-profile change of chief executive can have a big effect on the market's perception of a company and a change in FD (finance director) can signal that changes in operating procedures and profit structures are afoot. Needless to say, a company that changes its key personnel frequently is often a company in trouble which should be avoided.

PRR (price to research ratio): measures how research-minded a company is. To determine the PRR, divide the market cap by the total expenditure in research and development. The general idea is that a low PRR value can indicate that a company are trying to buy themselves a competitive edge but are presently undervalued. When using a company's PRR figure though you should be careful to compare like with like, since different sectors can require very different amounts of R & D.

PSR (price to sales ratio): this is found simply by dividing the current share price by the company's sales. A low PSR often implies that the company is undervalued but is shifting the goods; does this make it a good recovery ploy? The answer is that often it does, but that depends on profits and company debt as well.

PTBV (price to tangible book value): is worked out most easily by dividing the company's market cap by its (tangible) net assets. This determination only to include *tangible* assets and therefore to exclude things like patents and intellectual property rights provides a much harsher test of how much a company's assets really amount to. A low PTBV often indicates an undervalued company, but you should be clear that it's a one-dimensional measure and should not be used in isolation.

PW (profit warning): is issued by a company when it believes that its profits will be smaller than expected. Although most companies try to time a profit warning optimally to minimise damage, a profit warning can have a devastating effect on a company's share price.

QR (quick ratio): this measures what would happen if the company suddenly had to repay all of its current debts and liabilities and is calculated by dividing the current assets by the current debts. Though many companies can trade successfully with a quick ratio that is a good deal less than one, a low quick ratio (say below 0.4) means that there may be trouble in store and crises ahead; treat such businesses with caution.

REL STR (relative strength): is a measure of how well a share is performing relative to the rest of the market or a sector. A rise in relative strength indicates that the share is outperforming the market; a fall indicates that it is lagging behind. Looking at plots of the relative strength of a share basically saves having to compare the share price graphs with lots of others to see how well the share is doing.

ROCE (return on capital employed): tries to measure the 'competitive advantage' of a company. ROCE is calculated by expressing the pre-tax operating profit of a company as a percentage of the year-end capital employed in producing that profit. A ROCE value larger than 20 per cent usually indicates that the company has products that command a high return. Whether or not ROCE can be increased is also thought of as a measure of the efficiency of new management. Most important of all, a high ROCE value indicates that large proportions of the operating profit are available to be ploughed back into the company, fuelling even further growth.

SECT (sector): the sector of a share (usually) tells you what sort of business the company are engaged in. When the *Financial Times* lists share prices, it groups shares into sectors and then lists them alphabetically within those sectors. For example, in February 1999 there were nine companies in the 'Electricity' sector, the biggest being Scottish Power with a market cap of £7743 million and the smallest being Jersey Electricity Co. with a market cap of £16.9 million.

techMARK: is a technology index that was launched by the London Stock Exchange in November 1999 and includes around 200 companies already listed on the main market. It allows investors to track the performance of the UK technology sector using a single index.

TO (turnover): is simply the total sales of a company (not including any VAT) as reported in the announcements for next year or the annual report for last year. Obviously a high turnover is good as it means that the company is shifting lots of stock. But of course the real question is how much of the turnover is actually *profit*.

Volatility: measures how wild typical jumps in the share price are. AIM shares typically have high volatility and blue chips have low volatility. Although volatility may be calculated directly from a share price history, most option writers prefer to 'back it out' from somebody else's option valuation.

glossary of Internet terms

404: used to indicate an Internet user who is confused or generally lost. Comes from the '404 not found' error message indicating that a URL could not be located.

Acrobat: currently the only reliable way of viewing files of .pdf type. Down-loadable free from the Adobe home page.

ADSL: Asymmetrical Digital Subscriber Line. A high-speed communications line used mainly for digital video.

AFAIK: netspeak: 'As far as I know'.

AFAIR: netspeak: 'As far as I remember'.

Alpha geek: the local technical expert (usually not the computer manager) that people most often turn to when they have a problem.

AltaVista: one of the very best search engines.

Annie: an abandoned or 'orphaned' home page where nothing works.

Applet: a small JAVA program.

ARPANET: the genesis of the Internet: launched in the mid-1960s by the US Department of Defense as a series of protocols to allow different computers to talk to each other.

ASCII: American Standard Code for Information Interchange. Basic text with no control characters. All e-mail messages are sent in ASCII.

Bandwidth: the amount of information that may be sent through a connection. Usually measured in bits per second (BPS). If you don't have enough of it things will be slow.

BBS, Bulletin Board Service: an electronic meeting and announcement system that allows users to carry on discussions and upload and download files.

Bitnet: Because It's Time NET. An older network that connected academic IBM mainframes. Now being replaced by the Internet.

Bookmark: a convenient way of storing the URL of a frequently-visited web site.

BPS: bits per second. A measure of how fast data is moved around the net.

BRB, BBL: netspeak: 'Be right back', 'Be back later'.

Brownray: to replace a piece of software that works perfectly well with a newer version that doesn't work at all.

Browser: the software that allows you to navigate the world wide web and display web pages on your computer. Internet Explorer and Netscape are currently the two most popular varieties.

Bounce: what e-mail does when it cannot be delivered.

BTW: netspeak: 'By the way'.

Byte: a unit of computer memory large enough to hold one character of text.

Chat room: a location in cyberspace designed to host e-chat.

Cheese: content of a commercial site that consists mainly of glossy pictures of products or other generally useless information.

Cookie: a small piece of software that is downloaded from a website to your computer's hard drive which tells the webmaster things like your username, password(s) and other preferences. The idea is that this saves you from entering the same information time after time.

Cybercafe: an establishment offering coffee, tea and Internet access. Many have boomed but many have also gone bust.

Cyber-rattling: threats and generally angry words sent through cyberspace.

Cyberspace: where you are when you are accessing another system using your computer.

Daemon: a program running in background. For example, a program that keeps an IRC channel constantly open.

Domain name: the unique identifier of an Internet site. Domain names always have two or more parts separated by dots. Parts of the domain name identify the country (e.g. uk) and other parts identify the type of site (e.g. com=commercial, ac=academic, edu=US education, net=network, org=organization, gov=government, etc.).

Download: to receive and transfer information, data or files from another computer to your own.

E-mail: electronic mail. Messages, usually consisting of text (but often with encoded attachments) sent from one user to another via computer.

Emoticon: a combination of keyboard symbols used to show emotion, for example happy :-) sad :-(wink ;-).

Ethernet: a common method of networking computers in a LAN. Can handle about 10 million bits-per-second and may be used with almost any kind of computer.

FAQ: netspeak: 'Frequently asked questions'.

Firewall: a link in a network that is designed to prevent unauthorised users from accessing certain parts of the system.

Flaky: adjective applied to systems or software that are generally unreliable and crash frequently.

Flame: an e-mail that contains abusive, insulting or argumentative material.

Frames: an advanced feature of HTML that allows the screen to be broken up into independent regions. Some older browsers are not 'frames-enabled'.

Freeware: is free software.

FTP: file transfer protocol. The quickest and best way of using the net to transfer files from one computer to another.

FWIW: netspeak: 'For what it's worth' or alternatively 'For whatever it's worth'.

Gb, Gigabyte: 1000 megabytes (technically 1024 Mb).

GIF: graphical interchange format. A popular electronic image format.

GPRS: general packet radio service. Internet access from mobile phones has traditionally been very slow, but GPRS offers the promise of downloading web pages to your mobile at roughly the same speed as a domestic modem.

Hacker: criminal who tries to infiltrate other users' computers or systems, either to engage in criminal activities or just to annoy.

Hit counter: a piece of code that

counts how many times your web pages have been accessed by others. Usually provided free, but may give results of variable accuracy.

Home page: originally meant the web page that your browser points to when it fires up. More commonly now taken to mean the main web page for an individual, business or organisation.

Host: a computer on a network that serves as a repository for services available to other computers on the network.

HTML: HyperText Markup Language. The core programming language of web pages. To see what it looks like, use the 'view source' feature of your browser next time you're accessing somebody else's pages.

HTTP: HyperText Transfer Protocol. A new internet protocol that emerged in the early 1990s which has since become the industry standard.

Hyperlink: essentially an interactive table of contents that allows www users to jump around to various sections within a single document.

IE, Internet Explorer: the Microsoft standard browser.

IIRC: netspeak: 'If I remember correctly'.

IMO, IMHO: netspeak: 'In my opinion', 'In my humble opinion'.

Internet: officially the Internet (capital I) is the massive collection of inter-connected networks that all use TCP/IP protocols and form the web that we know and love. In contrast, an internet (lower case i) is simply the entity that results whenever two or more networks are connected together.

Intranet: a private network with restricted access. Uses similar software to the Internet but is for internal use only.

IP address: Internet Protocol address. A unique numerical identifier consisting of four groups of dot-separated numbers, for example 123.456.789.0. Every machine connected to the Internet has its own unique IP number.

IRC: Internet Relay Chat. A large multi-user chat facility run by a number of major servers.

ISP: an institution that provides access to the Internet in return for money or patronage.

Java: a programming language designed for networks to allow programs to be written that can be safely downloaded from the Internet.

JavaScript: JavaScript is a programming language that relies on the browser for interpretation when included in an HTML file. It's *not the same* as Java.

JPEG: Joint Photographic Experts Group. A popular and economical format for image files.

Kb, Kilobyte: 1000 bytes (technically 1024 bytes).

Kruegerapp: a downloaded application which promises to enhance your system performance but instead causes it to crash.

LAN: Local Area Network. A computer network limited to the immediate area (for example a particular building).

Links bar: a feature of most browsers that allows a user to easily access links that have previously been visited.

Linux: an increasingly popular operating system which is essentially free (you may have noticed that Microsoft's is not). Very net-friendly and much less flaky than Windows.

Mb, Megabyte: 1 million bytes. (Technically 1024 kilobytes.)

Mirror: an Internet site that maintains an exact copy of material which originates from another location. Usually set up to provide easier or more widespread access to a resource.

Modem: stands for MOdulator/DEModulator. A device that allows your computer to talk to other computers via a telephone line.

Netiquette: the art of behaving gracefully and altruistically on the net.

Net police: derogatory term for Internet users who take it upon themselves to impose their standards on every other Internet user.

Netscape: a widely-used browser which is seen as a viable alternative to Microsoft's Internet Explorer.

Network: two or more computers connected together in some way that allows them to share resources. Connected networks are an internet.

Newsgroup: a discussion area on USENET.

Node: any single computer connected to a network.

OCR: stands for Optical Character Recognition. A type of software that works with a scanner and allows printed or even handwritten text to be recognised and stored.

Offline: not connected to the Internet.

Plug-in: an item of software that adds features to a larger piece of software.

Port: a socket on a computer where information is transmitted or received.

Portal: essentially a marketing term to describe a website that is intended to catch the attention of www users. A point of entry site to the web.

Protocols: a set of rules that allow two computers to communicate with one another.

PSTN: stands for Public Switched Telephone Network but just means 'old-fashioned telephones'.

Public Key Encryption: a system for passing encrypted messages over the net that relies on the fact that finding the factors of large integers is a very hard thing for computers to do.

Router: a dedicated computer whose function is to handle connections between two or more networks.

Search engine: a site that allows users to search across the web for particular subjects, phrases or sentences. Included amongst the best sites are AltaVista, Lycos, Excite, Infoseek and Webcrawler.

Security certificate: a chunk of information (usually a text file) that the SSL protocol uses to establish a secure connection.

Server: a computer or a software package that provides a specific service to client software running on other computers.

Shareware: is software that may be obtained free in the first instance but is either not the full version of the program or requires a fee to be paid to its writer after a specific time has elapsed.

Shouting: Sending e-mail in capitals. Considered generally bad form.

SMDS: Switched Multimegabit Data Service. A new standard for very high-speed data transfer.

Smiley: same as emoticon (see above).

SMTP: Simple Mail Transfer Protocol. The primary protocol used for sending e-mail on the Internet. Basically a set of rules that govern how a mail sending program and a mail receiving program should interact.

Snail-mail: mail sent via the postal service (as opposed to e-mail).

Spamming: sending the same message unsolicited to an extremely large number of users. Highly annoying.

SSL: stands for Secure Sockets Layer. A protocol specifically designed by Netscape Communications to enable securely encrypted messages to be communicated across the Internet.

Sysop: (system operator) the person responsible for the physical operations of a computer system or network resource. Performs routine backup and maintenance tasks. A good person to be nice to.

T-3: a leased-line connection theoretically capable of carrying data at 44,736,000 BPS, which is fast enough for full-screen video.

Telnet: the command and the program that allows users to log in from one Internet site to another. Essential for logging in to your own computer from a remote host.

Terabyte: 1000 gigabytes.

Terminal: a device that allows users to send commands to a computer (which may or may not be elsewhere). Usually includes a keyboard, a screen and a mouse.

Terminal server: a special purpose computer equipped with ports to allow many modems to be connected. answers all calls and passes the connections on to the appropriate node.

TCP/IP: Transmission Control Protocol/Internet Protocol. The suite of protocols that essentially defines the Internet. Essential for Internet access.

UNIX: an operating system designed specifically for a multi-user environment. The most common operating system for Internet servers.

URL: Uniform Resource Locator. The standard form of address for Internet resources. Often begins http:// or ftp://.

USENET: a world-wide system of discussion groups where comments and e-chat are exchanged between millions of machines. Contains separate discussion areas called newsgroups.

UUENCODE: stands for Unix to Unix Encoding. A way of converting files from Binary to ASCII so that they can be e-mailed.

Virus: a piece of code deliberately designed to corrupt (or damage) people's systems which is unwittingly downloaded via e-mail or other data transfer mechanisms. Rarer than most people think, but can cause serious problems.

www: world wide web, but some (especially those with older modems) know it only as the world wide wait. Not actually synonymous with the Internet as the www is just one of the many services provided by the Internet.

XML: eXtensible Markup Language. The current favourite in the race to replace HTML as the standard programming language of the web.

Index

ProShare 83
prospectuses 201
protocols 278
PRR (price to research ratio) 270
PSR (price to sales ratio) 270
PSTN (Public Switched Telephone Network)
    278
PTBV (price to tangible book value) 270
public key encryption 62–3, 278
publications and books 259–63
put options 235

quality companies 95–6
quick ratio 271

record keeping 229
recording telephone calls 61
registers of shareholders 220
regulatory authorities 217–18
relative strength 103, 171–2, 271
reliability of service 31–2, 51
repeat purchases 149
research 26–7, 112–37
    accuracy of information 216–17
    annual reports 123–4, 176–7
    asking around 120–1
    books and publications 259–63
    charting 126–8, 179–81
    company visits 119–20
    company websites 121–3
    fundamentals of companies 113–19, 145,
        152–4, 157–8
    interpretation of terms 136
    newsletters/tip sheets 125–6
    share price monitoring 124–5
    television programmes 124
    website addresses 253–9
research and development spending 107
retirement 17–18
returns
    compound returns 18–20
    from blue chip companies 140–2

from building societies/deposit accounts 15
from gilts 15
from premium bonds 15
from property 15
from share trading 13–15
from traditional gambling 12–13
rights issues 56–7
Rio Tinto Zinc 149
risk assessment 65–6, 91, 225–6
ROCE (return on capital employed) 146, 149,
    176, 271
roulette 10, 12–13
routers 278
Royal & Sun Alliance 174

Safeway 144
Sainsbury's 144
Scholes, M. 241
schwab-worldwide.com 254
scrip issues 57–8
search engines 278
sector selection 85–6, 96–7, 177, 271–2
Securities Investor Protection Corporation
    (SIPC) 63–4
security 30, 59–66
    abnormal trading patterns 65
    and browser versions 66
    checking credentials of brokers 60
    electronic signatures 62–3
    encryption systems 62–3, 278
    firewalls 62, 275
    logging off 64–5
    passwords 41, 61, 224–5
    recording telephone calls 61
    risk assessment 65–6
    SIPC (Securities Investor Protection
        Corporation) 63–4
security certificates 278
selling decisions 80, 100–4
    cutting losses 221–2
    expected winnings calculations 104
    growth shares 178–82